Photographs on front cover and page 92 copyright © Shutterstock.com

Pictured on the front cover: Classic Apple Pie *(page 93)*.

Pictured on the back cover: *(clockwise from top left):* Chocolate-Cranberry Pumpkin Pancakes *(page 5)*, Lemon-Glazed Zucchini Muffins *(page 122)*, Pumpkin Swirl Brownies *(page 148)* and Ginger Plum Tart *(page 104)*.

ISBN: 978-1-64558-641-8

Manufactured in China.

8 7 6 5 4 3 2 1

Microwave Cooking: Microwave ovens vary in wattage. Use the cooking times as guidelines and check for doneness before adding more time.

Let's get social!

⊙ @Publications_International

𝕗 @PublicationsInternational

www.pilbooks.com

TABLE OF CONTENTS

BOUNTIFUL BREAKFASTS

CHOCOLATE-CRANBERRY PUMPKIN PANCAKES

2 cups all-purpose flour

⅓ cup packed brown sugar

2 teaspoons baking powder

½ teaspoon salt

½ teaspoon ground cinnamon

¼ teaspoon baking soda

¼ teaspoon ground ginger

¼ teaspoon ground nutmeg

1½ cups milk

2 eggs

½ cup canned pumpkin

¼ cup canola or vegetable oil

½ cup mini semisweet chocolate chips

½ cup dried cranberries

⅓ cup cinnamon chips*

1 to 2 teaspoons butter, plus additional for serving

Maple syrup

*If cinnamon chips are not available, substitute an additional ⅓ cup mini chocolate chips.

1. Combine flour, brown sugar, baking powder, salt, cinnamon, baking soda, ginger and nutmeg in large bowl; mix well. Beat milk, eggs, pumpkin and oil in medium bowl until well blended. Add to flour mixture with chocolate chips, cranberries and cinnamon chips; stir just until dry ingredients are moistened.

2. Heat 1 teaspoon butter on griddle or in large nonstick skillet over medium heat. Pour batter by ¼ cupfuls onto griddle. Cook until bubbles form and bottoms of pancakes are lightly browned; turn and cook 2 minutes or until browned and cooked through. Repeat with remaining batter, adding additional butter to griddle if necessary. Serve with maple syrup and additional butter, if desired.

Makes 16 to 18 (4-inch) pancakes

WALNUT-CRANBERRY TWIST DANISH

2¾ to 3¼ cups all-purpose flour, divided

1 package (¼ ounce) active dry yeast

½ teaspoon ground allspice

¾ cup milk

¼ cup plus 2 tablespoons granulated sugar, divided

2 tablespoons butter

1 teaspoon salt

1 egg

1 cup chopped fresh or frozen cranberries

¼ cup chopped walnuts

1 tablespoon powdered sugar

1. Combine 1 cup flour, yeast and allspice in large mixing bowl. Heat milk, 2 tablespoons granulated sugar, butter and salt to 120° to 130°F in small saucepan. Add milk mixture and egg to flour mixture. Beat with electric mixer on low speed 1 minute. Increase speed to high; beat 3 minutes.

2. Stir in 1¾ cups flour. Attach dough hook to mixer; knead on medium-low speed 3 to 5 minutes or until dough is smooth and elastic, adding enough remaining flour to make soft dough. Shape dough into a ball. Place in large lightly greased bowl; turn to grease top. Cover and let rise in warm place about 1 hour or until doubled in size.

3. Meanwhile, stir together cranberries, walnuts and remaining ¼ cup granulated sugar in small bowl.

4. Lightly grease baking sheet. Turn out dough onto lightly floured surface. Roll dough into 16×10-inch rectangle Spread cranberry mixture over dough. Starting from long side, roll up dough. Pinch seam to seal. Turn roll seam side down. Cut roll in half lengthwise. Loosely twist roll halves together on prepared baking sheet, keeping cut sides up. Pinch ends to seal. Loosely cover with plastic wrap. Let rise in warm place about 30 minutes or until doubled in size.

5. Preheat oven to 350°F. Bake about 25 minutes or until lightly browned, covering with foil during last 5 minutes to prevent overbrowning if necessary. Remove bread to wire rack; cool completely. Sprinkle with powdered sugar.

Makes 1 loaf

FRESH PLUM COFFEECAKE

2¼ cups all-purpose flour, divided

¼ cup packed brown sugar

½ teaspoon ground cinnamon

1 tablespoon butter, softened

1½ teaspoons baking powder

½ teaspoon baking soda

½ teaspoon salt

1 cup lemon or plain yogurt

⅔ cup granulated sugar

2 egg whites

1 egg

1 teaspoon grated lemon peel

4 medium plums, cut into ¼-inch-thick slices

1. Preheat oven to 350°F. Spray 9-inch square pan with nonstick cooking spray.

2. For topping, combine ¼ cup flour, brown sugar, cinnamon and butter in small bowl with fork until crumbs form; set aside.

3. Combine remaining 2 cups flour, baking powder, baking soda and salt in medium bowl. Whisk yogurt, granulated sugar, egg whites, egg and lemon peel in large bowl until well blended. Add to flour mixture; mix just until dry ingredients are moistened.

4. Pour batter into prepared pan. Arrange plums over batter; sprinkle evenly with reserved topping. Bake 30 to 35 minutes or until toothpick inserted into center comes out clean. Cool in pan on wire rack. Serve warm or at room temperature.

Makes 9 servings

APPLE CREAM CHEESE BREAKFAST BARS

Crust

- **1** package (about 15 ounces) yellow cake mix
- **¼** teaspoon grated lemon peel
- **½** cup (1 stick) butter, softened

Filling

- **12** ounces cream cheese, softened
- **½** cup sugar
- **2** eggs
- **½** cup half-and-half
- **2** teaspoons vanilla

Topping

- **⅓** cup sugar
- **1** teaspoon ground cinnamon
- **1** teaspoon ground nutmeg
- **¼** teaspoon grated lemon peel
- **2½** cups thinly sliced peeled Granny Smith apples (about 2 medium)
- **½** cup sliced almonds

1. Preheat oven to 350°F. For crust, combine cake mix and ¼ teaspoon lemon peel in large bowl. Reserve ½ cup mixture; set aside. Add butter to remaining mixture; beat with electric mixer at low speed until crumbly. Press mixture onto bottom and up sides of ungreased 13×9-inch baking pan. Bake 10 minutes or until lightly browned.

2. For filling, beat cream cheese and reserved ½ cup cake mix in large bowl with electric mixer on medium speed until well blended. Gradually add ½ cup sugar; beat until creamy. Add eggs, one at a time, beating well after each addition. Stir in half-and-half and vanilla until well blended. Pour into baked crust.

3. For topping, combine ⅓ cup sugar, cinnamon, nutmeg and remaining ¼ teaspoon lemon peel in large bowl. Add apples; toss to coat. Spoon apple mixture over cream cheese layer; sprinkle with almonds.

4. Bake 30 to 35 minutes or until center is set. Cool completely in pan on wire rack. Cut into bars. Store leftovers in refrigerator.

Makes 18 bars

ZUCCHINI BREAD PANCAKES

- 2 **medium zucchini**
- ½ **cup vanilla or plain yogurt**
- 2 **eggs**
- ¼ **cup milk**
- 2 **tablespoons canola or vegetable oil**
- 1 **cup whole wheat flour**
- ¼ **cup packed brown sugar**
- 2 **teaspoons grated lemon peel**
- 2 **teaspoons baking soda**
- 1 **teaspoon ground cinnamon**
- ½ **teaspoon salt**
- ¼ **teaspoon ground nutmeg**
- 1 **to 2 teaspoons butter, plus additional for serving**
  Maple syrup

1. Grate zucchini on large holes of box grater; place in large bowl. Add yogurt, eggs, milk and oil; mix well. Add flour, brown sugar, lemon peel, baking soda, cinnamon, salt and nutmeg; stir just until combined.

2. Heat 1 teaspoon butter on large nonstick griddle or in large nonstick skillet over medium heat. Pour batter by ¼ cupfuls of batter onto griddle. Cook until bubbles form and bottoms of pancakes are lightly browned; turn and cook 2 minutes or until browned and cooked through. Repeat with 1 teaspoon butter and remaining batter.

3. Serve with maple syrup and additional butter.

Makes 12 (4-inch) pancakes

BAKED PUMPKIN OATMEAL

2 cups old-fashioned oats

2 cups milk

1 cup canned pumpkin

2 eggs

⅓ cup packed brown sugar

1 teaspoon vanilla

½ cup dried cranberries, plus additional for topping

1 teaspoon pumpkin pie spice

½ teaspoon salt

½ teaspoon baking powder

Maple syrup

Chopped pecans (optional)

1. Preheat oven to 350°F. Spray 8-inch square baking dish with nonstick cooking spray.

2. Spread oats on ungreased baking sheet. Bake 10 minutes or until fragrant and lightly browned, stirring occasionally. Pour into medium bowl; let cool slightly.

3. Whisk milk, pumpkin, eggs, brown sugar and vanilla in large bowl until well blended. Add ½ cup cranberries, pumpkin pie spice, salt and baking powder to oats; mix well. Add oat mixture to pumpkin mixture; stir until well blended. Pour into prepared baking dish.

4. Bake 45 minutes or until set and knife inserted into center comes out almost clean. Serve warm with maple syrup, additional cranberries and pecans, if desired.

Makes 6 servings

APPLE RING COFFEECAKE

3 cups all-purpose flour	1 cup vegetable oil
1 teaspoon baking soda	2 eggs
1 teaspoon salt	2 teaspoons vanilla
1 teaspoon ground cinnamon	2 medium tart apples, peeled, cored and chopped
1 cup chopped walnuts	
1½ cups granulated sugar	Powdered sugar (optional)

1. Preheat oven to 325°F. Grease 10-inch tube pan.

2. Whisk flour, baking soda, salt and cinnamon in large bowl until well blended. Stir in walnuts.

3. Combine granulated sugar, oil, eggs and vanilla in medium bowl. Stir in apples. Stir into flour mixture just until moistened.

4. Spoon batter into prepared pan, spreading evenly. Bake 1 hour or until toothpick inserted near center comes out clean. Cool cake in pan on wire rack 10 minutes. Loosen edges with metal spatula, if necessary. Remove from pan; cool completely on wire rack.

5. Sprinkle with powdered sugar just before serving, if desired.

Makes 12 servings

SWEET POTATO PANCAKES

Pancakes

- 2 medium sweet potatoes
- 2½ cups all-purpose flour
- 1 teaspoon baking powder
- 1 teaspoon baking soda
- ½ teaspoon salt
- ½ teaspoon ground cinnamon
- ¼ teaspoon ground ginger
- 2¾ cups buttermilk
- 2 eggs
- 2 tablespoons packed brown sugar
- 2 tablespoons butter, melted, plus additional for pan

Ginger Butter

- ¼ cup (½ stick) butter, softened
- 1 tablespoon packed brown sugar
- 1 teaspoon grated fresh ginger
- Pinch of salt
- Warm caramel sauce or maple syrup
- ¾ cup chopped glazed pecans* (optional)

*Glazed or candied pecans may be found in the produce section of the supermarket or in the snack aisle.

1. Preheat oven to 375°F. Scrub sweet potatoes; bake 50 to 60 minutes or until soft. Cool slightly; peel and mash. Measure out 1⅓ cups for pancake batter.

2. Combine flour, baking powder, baking soda, ½ teaspoon salt, cinnamon and ground ginger in medium bowl; mix well. Whisk buttermilk, eggs and 2 tablespoons brown sugar in large bowl. Stir in 2 tablespoons melted butter. Add sweet potatoes; whisk until well blended. Add flour mixture; stir just until dry ingredients are moistened. Batter will be lumpy; do not overmix. Let stand 10 minutes.

3. Heat griddle or large skillet* over medium heat; brush with butter to coat. For each pancake, pour ½ cup of batter onto griddle, spreading into 5- to 6-inch circle. Cook about 4 minutes or until bottom is golden brown and small bubbles appear on surface. Turn pancake; cook about 3 minutes or until golden brown. Add additional butter to griddle as needed. Repeat with additional batter.

4. For ginger butter, beat softened butter, 1 tablespoon brown sugar, fresh ginger and pinch of salt in small bowl until well blended.

5. Serve pancakes with ginger butter, caramel sauce and pecans, if desired.

*Pancakes are large and a skillet may not be able to cook more than one at a time. Keep pancakes warm in 250°F oven on wire rack set over baking sheet. Or use ¼ cup batter per pancake for smaller pancakes.

Makes 10 large pancakes (5 servings)

APRICOT SPICE COFFEECAKE

1 cup whole wheat flour

½ teaspoon baking soda

½ teaspoon ground cinnamon

¼ teaspoon salt

½ cup buttermilk

¼ cup packed brown sugar

2 tablespoons canola or vegetable oil

1 egg

1 teaspoon vanilla

1 can (15 ounces) apricot halves in juice, drained

1 tablespoon old-fashioned oats

¼ cup powdered sugar

1 to 2 teaspoons milk

1. Preheat oven to 350°F. Spray 8- or 9-inch round cake pan with nonstick cooking spray.

2. Whisk flour, baking soda, cinnamon and salt in small bowl until well blended. Whisk buttermilk, brown sugar, oil, egg and vanilla in large bowl until smooth and well blended. Stir in flour mixture just until moistened. Pour batter into prepared pan. Arrange apricot halves, cut side down, over batter. Sprinkle evenly with oats.

3. Bake 27 to 30 minutes or until golden brown and top springs back when touched in center. Cool in pan on wire rack 10 minutes.

4. Whisk powdered sugar and 1 teaspoon milk in small bowl until blended. Add additional milk, if necessary, until desired consistency is reached. Drizzle over coffeecake. Serve warm.

Makes 10 servings

BAKED APPLE PANCAKE

- 3 tablespoons butter
- 3 medium Granny Smith apples (about 1¼ pounds), peeled and cut into ¼-inch slices
- ½ cup packed dark brown sugar
- 1½ teaspoons ground cinnamon
- ½ teaspoon plus pinch of salt, divided

- 4 eggs
- ⅓ cup whipping cream
- ⅓ cup milk
- 2 tablespoons granulated sugar
- ½ teaspoon vanilla
- ⅔ cup all-purpose flour

1. Melt butter in 8-inch ovenproof nonstick or cast iron skillet over medium heat. Add apples, brown sugar, cinnamon and pinch of salt; cook 8 minutes or until apples begin to soften, stirring occasionally. Spread apples in even layer in skillet; set aside to cool 30 minutes.

2. After apples have cooled 30 minutes, preheat oven to 425°F. Whisk eggs in large bowl until foamy. Add cream, milk, granulated sugar, vanilla and remaining ½ teaspoon salt; whisk until blended. Sift flour into egg mixture; whisk until batter is well blended and smooth. Set aside 15 minutes.

3. Stir batter; pour evenly over apple mixture. Place skillet on rimmed baking sheet in case of drips (or place baking sheet or piece of foil in oven beneath skillet).

4. Bake 16 minutes or until top is golden brown and pancake is loose around edge. Cool 1 minute; loosen edge of pancake with spatula, if necessary. Place large serving plate or cutting board on top of skillet and invert pancake onto plate. Serve warm.

Makes 2 to 4 servings

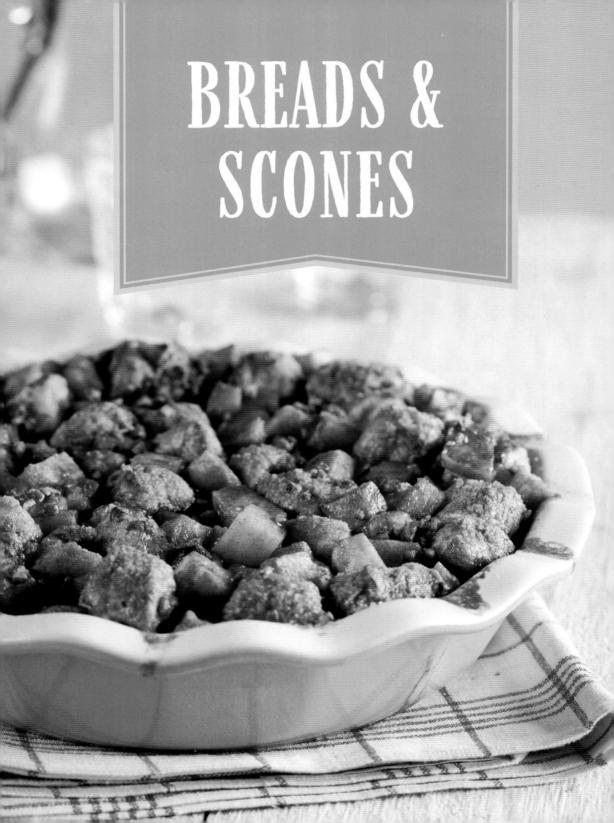

BREADS & SCONES

APPLE PIE MONKEY BREAD

- ½ **cup (1 stick) butter, divided**
- 2 **large apples (about 1 pound), peeled and cut into ½-inch pieces (Fuji, Granny Smith or Braeburn)**
- ½ **cup plus 1 tablespoon sugar, divided**
- 2½ **teaspoons ground cinnamon, divided**
- ½ **cup finely chopped pecans**
- 2 **packages (7½ ounces each) refrigerated buttermilk biscuits (10 biscuits per package)**

1. Preheat oven to 350°F. Spray 9-inch deep-dish pie plate with nonstick cooking spray.

2. Melt ¼ cup butter in large skillet or saucepan over medium heat. Add apples, 1 tablespoon sugar and ½ teaspoon cinnamon; cook and stir 5 minutes or until apples are tender and glazed. Transfer to large bowl. Melt remaining ¼ cup butter in same skillet, stirring to scrape up any glaze. Cool slightly.

3. Combine pecans, remaining ½ cup sugar and 2 teaspoons cinnamon in medium bowl. Separate biscuits; cut each biscuit into four pieces with scissors. Dip biscuit pieces in melted butter; roll in pecan mixture to coat. Place one quarter of biscuit pieces in prepared pie plate; top with one quarter of apples. Repeat layers three times. Sprinkle with remaining pecan mixture and drizzle with remaining butter.

4. Bake 30 minutes or until biscuits are firm and topping is golden brown. Serve warm.

Makes about 12 servings

PUMPKIN-GINGER SCONES

½ **cup sugar, divided**

2 **cups all-purpose flour**

2 **teaspoons baking powder**

1 **teaspoon ground cinnamon**

½ **teaspoon baking soda**

½ **teaspoon salt**

¼ **cup (½ stick) cold butter, cut into small pieces**

1 **egg**

½ **cup canned pumpkin**

¼ **cup sour cream**

½ **teaspoon grated fresh ginger *or* 2 tablespoons finely chopped crystallized ginger**

1 **tablespoon butter, melted**

1. Preheat oven to 425°F.

2. Reserve 1 tablespoon sugar; combine remaining sugar, flour, baking powder, cinnamon, baking soda and salt in large bowl. Cut in ¼ cup butter with pastry blender or use electric mixer on low speed until mixture resembles coarse crumbs. Whisk egg in medium bowl. Add pumpkin, sour cream and ginger; whisk until well blended. Add to flour mixture; stir until soft dough forms.

3. Turn dough out onto well-floured surface. Knead 10 times. Pat dough into 9×6-inch rectangle or roll with floured rolling pin. Cut into six 3-inch squares. Cut each square diagonally in half, making 12 triangles; place 2 inches apart on ungreased baking sheets. Brush tops of triangles with melted butter and sprinkle with reserved 1 tablespoon sugar.

4. Bake 10 to 12 minutes or until golden brown. Remove to wire racks; cool 10 minutes. Serve warm.

Makes 12 scones

APRICOT-CRANBERRY BREAD

2½ cups all-purpose flour

4 teaspoons baking powder

½ teaspoon baking soda

½ teaspoon salt

1¼ cups buttermilk

¾ cup sugar

¼ cup (½ stick) butter, melted or vegetable oil

1 egg

1 cup chopped dried apricots

½ cup dried cranberries

1. Preheat oven to 350°F. Spray 9×5-inch loaf pan with nonstick cooking spray.

2. Whisk flour, baking powder, baking soda and salt in large bowl. Whisk buttermilk, sugar, butter and egg in medium bowl; stir into flour mixture just until dry ingredients are moistened. Stir in apricots and cranberries. Pour batter into prepared pan; smooth top.

3. Bake 45 to 50 minutes or until toothpick inserted into center comes out clean. Cool in pan on wire rack 10 minutes. Remove from pan; cool completely.

Makes 1 loaf

MAPLE-PUMPKIN-PECAN TWIST

Bread

- ¾ cup warm water (110°F)
- 1 package (¼ ounce; 2¼ teaspoons) active dry yeast
- ½ cup granulated sugar
- ½ cup canned pumpkin
- 2 eggs
- ¼ cup (½ stick) butter, melted, or vegetable oil
- 1½ teaspoons salt
- 1½ teaspoons maple flavoring or vanilla
- 4½ cups all-purpose flour, divided
- 1 cup coarsely chopped pecans

Maple Glaze

- 1¼ cups powdered sugar
- ¼ cup milk
- 1 teaspoon maple flavoring or vanilla

1. Stir water and yeast in large bowl of stand mixer until yeast is dissolved; let stand 5 minutes. Stir in granulated sugar, pumpkin, eggs, butter, salt and 1½ teaspoons maple flavoring; mix well. Add 4¼ cups flour and pecans; knead with dough hook on medium-low speed 5 to 7 minutes or until dough is smooth, adding additional flour 1 tablespoon at a time if needed for dough to clean side of bowl. Dough will be sticky. Place dough in large lightly greased bowl; turn to grease top. Cover and let rise in warm place 1 hour 30 minutes or until dough is puffy (it may not double in size).

2. Line baking sheet with parchment paper or lightly grease. Punch down dough; turn out onto floured surface. Divide dough in half; roll each half into 24-inch rope. Twist ropes together and place on prepared baking sheet; shape into 10-inch ring shape and pinch ends to seal. Cover with clean kitchen towel; let rise in warm place 45 minutes or until puffy.

3. Preheat oven to 375°F. Bake 25 to 30 minutes or until golden brown. Immediately remove from baking sheet; cool on wire rack.

4. For glaze, whisk powdered sugar, milk and 1 teaspoon maple flavoring in small bowl until smooth. Drizzle over loaf.

Makes 1 loaf

CHOCOLATE CHIP ZUCCHINI BREAD

2 **small zucchini**	1 **small seedless orange**
2 **cups sugar**	2 **cups all-purpose flour**
1 **cup (2 sticks) butter, melted**	1 **teaspoon baking soda**
3 **eggs**	1 **teaspoon salt**
⅓ **cup unsweetened cocoa powder**	1 **teaspoon ground cinnamon**
1 **teaspoon vanilla**	¾ **cup semisweet chocolate chips**

1. Preheat oven to 350°F. Lightly grease two 9×5-inch loaf pans.

2. Grate zucchini on large holes of box grater; squeeze dry and place in large bowl. Add sugar, butter, eggs, cocoa and vanilla; stir until well blended.

3. Cut orange into wedges. Place orange (including peel) in food processor; process until finely ground (including peel). Stir into zucchini mixture. Stir in flour, baking soda, salt and cinnamon. Fold in chocolate chips. Pour batter into loaf pans.

4. Bake 1 hour or until toothpick inserted into centers of loaves comes out clean. Cool in pans 10 minutes; remove to wire rack. Cool 1 hour before slicing.

Makes 2 loaves

APPLE-CHEDDAR SCONES

1 cup all-purpose flour

1 cup white whole wheat flour

3 tablespoons sugar

1½ teaspoons baking powder

½ teaspoon salt

½ teaspoon ground cinnamon

¼ teaspoon baking soda

1 Granny Smith apple, peeled and diced

½ cup (2 ounces) shredded sharp Cheddar cheese

⅓ cup unsweetened applesauce

1 egg

¼ cup milk or whipping cream

5 tablespoons melted butter, divided

1. Preheat oven to 425°F. Line baking sheet with parchment paper.

2. Combine all-purpose flour, white whole wheat flour, sugar, baking powder, salt, cinnamon and baking soda in large bowl; mix well. Stir in apple and cheese until well blended.

3. Whisk applesauce, egg, milk and 4 tablespoons butter in small bowl until smooth and well blended. Stir into flour mixture until moistened. (Dough will be sticky.)

4. Knead dough on floured surface five times; pat into 8-inch circle. Cut into eight wedges; place on prepared baking sheet. Brush tops with remaining 1 tablespoon butter.

5. Bake 15 minutes or until lightly golden. Remove to wire rack; serve warm or cool completely.

Makes 8 scones

PUMPKIN BREAD

2¼	cups all-purpose flour	1	cup granulated sugar
1	tablespoon pumpkin pie spice	1	cup packed brown sugar
1	teaspoon baking powder	⅔	cup canola or vegetable oil
1	teaspoon baking soda	1	teaspoon vanilla
¾	teaspoon salt	¼	cup roasted salted pumpkin seeds, coarsely chopped or crushed
3	eggs		
1	can (15 ounces) pumpkin		

1. Preheat oven to 350°F. Spray two 8×4-inch loaf pans with nonstick cooking spray.

2. Combine flour, pumpkin pie spice, baking powder, baking soda and salt in medium bowl; mix well.

3. Beat eggs in large bowl. Add pumpkin, granulated sugar, brown sugar, oil and vanilla; whisk until well blended. Add flour mixture; stir just until dry ingredients are moistened. Divide batter between prepared pans; smooth tops. Sprinkle with pumpkin seeds; pat seeds gently into batter to adhere.

4. Bake about 50 minutes or until toothpick inserted into centers comes out mostly clean with just a few moist crumbs. Cool in pans 10 minutes; remove to wire racks to cool completely.

Makes 2 loaves

NOTE: The recipe can be made in one 9×5-inch loaf pan instead of two 8×4-inch pans. Bake about 1 hour 20 minutes or until toothpick inserted into center comes out with just a few moist crumbs. Check bread after 50 minutes; cover loosely with foil if top is browning too quickly.

CLASSIC ZUCCHINI BREAD

2 cups all-purpose flour	½ cup canola or vegetable oil
1 teaspoon salt	2 eggs
1 teaspoon ground cinnamon	½ cup granulated sugar
¾ teaspoon baking powder	½ cup packed brown sugar
¾ teaspoon baking soda	1 teaspoon vanilla
¼ teaspoon ground nutmeg	2 cups packed grated zucchini (2 to 3 medium)

1. Preheat oven to 350°F. Spray 9×5-inch loaf pan with nonstick cooking spray or line with parchment paper.

2. Combine flour, salt, cinnamon, baking powder, baking soda and nutmeg in medium bowl; mix well. Beat oil, eggs, granulated sugar, brown sugar and vanilla in large bowl until well blended. Add flour mixture; stir just until dry ingredients are moistened. Stir in zucchini until blended. Pour batter into prepared pan; smooth top.

3. Bake 55 to 60 minutes or until toothpick inserted into center comes out clean. Cool in pan 20 minutes; remove to wire rack to cool completely.

Makes 1 loaf

SPICED PUMPKIN BEER BREAD

2¼ cups all-purpose flour	1½ cups sugar
2 teaspoons baking powder	1¼ cups canned pumpkin
1 teaspoon ground cinnamon	¾ cup lager
¾ teaspoon baking soda	½ cup canola or vegetable oil
½ teaspoon salt	2 eggs
¼ teaspoon ground nutmeg	½ cup coarsely chopped walnuts
⅛ teaspoon ground cloves	

1. Preheat oven to 350°F. Grease and flour 9×5-inch loaf pan.

2. Whisk flour, baking powder, cinnamon, baking soda, salt, nutmeg and cloves in large bowl until well blended. Combine sugar, pumpkin, lager, oil and eggs in medium bowl; beat until well blended. Add to flour mixture; stir just until dry ingredients are moistened. Stir in walnuts. Pour batter into prepared pan; smooth top.

3. Bake about 1 hour or until toothpick inserted into center comes out clean. Cool in pan 10 minutes; remove to wire rack. Cool 1 hour before serving.

Makes 1 loaf

CAKES & CHEESECAKES

CINNAMON PECAN PUMPKIN CAKE

- 2 cups all-purpose flour
- 1 cup granulated sugar
- ¾ cup packed dark brown sugar
- 2 teaspoons baking powder
- 2 teaspoons pumpkin pie spice
- 1 teaspoon salt
- 1 can (15 ounces) pumpkin
- ½ cup canola or vegetable oil
- ½ cup milk
- 2 eggs
- 1 teaspoon vanilla
- ¾ cup cinnamon chips, divided*
- ½ cup chopped pecans, divided

*If cinnamon chips are not available, substitute butterscotch or white chocolate chips.

1. Preheat oven to 350°F. Grease 13×9-inch baking pan or line with parchment paper.

2. Combine flour, granulated sugar, brown sugar, baking powder, pumpkin pie spice and salt in large bowl; mix well, breaking up any lumps of brown sugar. Whisk pumpkin, oil, milk, eggs and vanilla in medium bowl. Add to flour mixture; stir just until dry ingredients are moistened. Stir in ½ cup cinnamon chips and ¼ cup pecans. Spread batter in prepared pan; sprinkle with remaining cinnamon chips and pecans.

3. Bake 25 to 30 minutes or until toothpick inserted into center comes out clean. Cool in pan at least 15 minutes before serving. Cake is best the day it's made.

Makes 12 to 16 servings

TARTE TATIN

1 cup all-purpose flour	½ cup granulated sugar
Grated peel of 1 lemon	½ cup (1 stick) butter, melted
¼ teaspoon salt	½ cup dark brown sugar, loosely packed
4 tablespoons cold butter	1 tablespoon Calvados or other apple brandy
2 to 3 tablespoons ice water	Sweetened whipped cream (optional)
8 Granny Smith apples (about 3 pounds)	

1. Combine flour, lemon peel and salt in large bowl. Cut in cold butter with pastry blender or use electric mixer on low speed until mixture resembles coarse crumbs. Sprinkle mixture with ice water, 1 tablespoon at a time. Toss with fork until mixture holds together. Press together to form ball; shape into 6-inch disc. Wrap dough in plastic wrap; refrigerate at least 30 minutes.

2. Preheat oven to 375°F. Peel and core apples; cut into halves. Place apple halves, core sides up, in 13×9-inch baking dish. Sprinkle with granulated sugar. Bake 45 minutes; remove from oven. *Increase oven temperature to 425°F.*

3. Roll out dough on lightly floured surface with lightly floured rolling pin into circle at least 1 inch larger than inverted 9-inch pie plate.

4. Pour melted butter into 9-inch pie pan. Quickly spread brown sugar over butter. Sprinkle with Calvados. Arrange cooked apples, core sides up, in concentric circles. Carefully lift dough and place over apples. Gently press dough around fruit. Trim crust even with edge of pie plate. Turn under edge of crust to seal. Prick several holes in crust with fork to release steam.

5. Bake 20 to 25 minutes until crust is golden brown and apples are tender. Let tart stand 10 minutes before inverting onto serving platter. Garnish with whipped cream, if desired. Serve immediately.

Makes 8 servings

APPLE-PECAN CHEESECAKE

2 packages (8 ounces each) cream cheese, softened

⅔ cup sugar, divided

2 eggs

½ teaspoon vanilla

1 (9-inch) prepared graham cracker crust

½ teaspoon ground cinnamon

4 cups Golden Delicious or Granny Smith apples, peeled, cored and thinly sliced (about 2½ pounds apples)

½ cup chopped pecans

1. Preheat oven to 350°F.

2. Beat cream cheese and ⅓ cup sugar in large bowl with electric mixer at medium speed until well blended. Add eggs, one at a time, beating well after each addition. Blend in vanilla; pour into crust.

3. Combine remaining ⅓ cup sugar and cinnamon in large bowl. Add apples; toss gently to coat. Arrange apple mixture over cream cheese mixture. Sprinkle with pecans.

4. Bake 1 hour and 10 minutes or until set. Cool completely. Store in refrigerator.

Makes 10 to 12 servings

BANANA PECAN BUNDT CAKE WITH BUTTER SAUCE

½ cup (1 stick) plus 2 tablespoons butter, divided

1 cup chopped pecans, toasted*

1 package (about 15 ounces) yellow cake mix

1⅓ cups water

5 eggs

¾ cup mashed ripe bananas (2 medium bananas)**

½ cup puréed drained canned or cooked sweet potatoes

2 tablespoons vegetable oil

¾ cup sugar

¼ cup apple cider, apple juice or bourbon

¼ cup milk

*To toast pecans, spread on baking sheet. Bake in preheated 350°F oven 8 to 10 minutes or until golden brown, stirring frequently.

**Do not use overripe bananas.

1. Preheat oven to 325°F. Grease 12-cup (10-inch) bundt pan with 2 tablespoons butter. Sprinkle pecans evenly in bottom of pan.

2. Combine cake mix, water, eggs, bananas, sweet potatoes and oil in large bowl; beat with electric mixer at low speed 30 seconds. Beat at medium speed 2 minutes. Pour batter into prepared pan.

3. Bake 55 to 60 minutes or until toothpick inserted into center comes out clean. Cool in pan on wire rack 15 minutes. Gently loosen side and center of cake with knife; invert onto wire rack to cool completely.

4. Combine sugar, remaining ½ cup butter, apple cider and milk in small saucepan; cook and stir over medium-high heat until butter is melted and sugar is dissolved. Cut cake into slices; top with warm sauce.

Makes 10 to 12 servings

AUTUMN DUMP CAKE

1   can (29 ounces) pear pieces
    in light syrup, undrained

1   can (21 ounces) apple pie
    filling

½   cup dried cranberries

1   package (about 15 ounces)
    yellow cake mix

½   cup (1 stick) butter, cut into
    thin slices

¼   cup caramel topping,
    warmed

1. Preheat oven to 350°F. Spray 13×9-inch baking pan with nonstick cooking spray.

2. Drain pears, reserving ½ cup syrup. Spread pears and apple pie filling in prepared pan; drizzle with reserved pear syrup. Sprinkle with cranberries. Top with cake mix, spreading evenly. Top with butter in single layer, covering cake mix as much as possible. Drizzle with caramel topping.

3. Bake 40 to 45 minutes or until toothpick inserted into center of cake comes out clean. Cool at least 15 minutes before serving.

Makes 12 to 16 servings

PLUM CAKE WITH STREUSEL TOPPING

Streusel Topping

- ¼ **cup all-purpose flour**
- 3 **tablespoons packed brown sugar**
- ½ **teaspoon ground cinnamon**
- 2 **tablespoons butter, softened**

Cake

- 1 **cup plus 2 tablespoons all-purpose flour**
- ½ **teaspoon baking powder**
- ¼ **teaspoon baking soda**
- ¼ **teaspoon salt**
- 6 **tablespoons (¾ stick) butter, softened**
- ¼ **cup granulated sugar**
- ¼ **cup packed brown sugar**
- 1 **teaspoon vanilla**
- 2 **eggs**
- ¼ **cup buttermilk**
- 3 **medium plums, pitted and each cut into 8 wedges***

*Plums should be underripe and slightly soft to the touch.

1. Preheat oven to 350°F. Spray 9-inch springform pan with nonstick cooking spray. Line bottom of pan with parchment paper; spray parchment paper with cooking spray. For topping, combine ¼ cup flour, 3 tablespoons packed brown sugar and ½ teaspoon cinnamon in medium bowl. Mix in 2 tablespoons butter with fingers until crumbly.

2. For cake, combine 1 cup plus 2 tablespoons flour, baking powder, baking soda and salt in medium bowl.

3. Beat 6 tablespoons butter in large bowl with electric mixer at medium speed 1 minute. Add granulated sugar and ¼ cup brown sugar; beat 1 minute or until light and fluffy. Beat in vanilla. Add eggs, one at a time, beating well after each addition. Alternately add flour mixture and buttermilk, beating well at low speed after each addition.

4. Spread batter in prepared pan. Arrange plum wedges on top of batter. Sprinkle with topping.

5. Bake 30 minutes or until cake springs back when lightly touched. Remove to wire rack. Remove side of pan; cool 20 minutes. Slide spatula under cake to transfer to serving plate. Serve warm or at room temperature.

Makes 8 servings

BUTTERSCOTCH MALT ZUCCHINI CAKE

½ cup (1 stick) plus
   2 tablespoons butter,
   softened, divided

2½ cups all-purpose flour

¼ cup malted milk powder

1 teaspoon baking soda

½ teaspoon salt

½ teaspoon baking powder

½ teaspoon ground nutmeg

1¾ cups packed brown sugar

½ cup canola or vegetable oil

2 eggs

½ cup buttermilk

1 teaspoon vanilla

2 cups grated zucchini

¾ cup white chocolate chips,
   divided

¾ cup butterscotch chips,
   divided

½ cup chopped walnuts or
   pecans

1. Preheat oven to 350°F. Grease 12-cup (10-inch) bundt pan with 2 tablespoons butter; dust with flour.

2. Whisk flour, malted milk powder, baking soda, salt, baking powder and nutmeg in medium bowl until well blended.

3. Beat brown sugar, remaining ½ cup butter, oil and eggs in large bowl with electric mixer at medium speed 2 minutes. Add buttermilk and vanilla; beat until well blended. Add flour mixture; mix at low speed just until blended. Stir in zucchini, ½ cup white chocolate chips, ½ cup butterscotch chips and chopped nuts. Pour into prepared pan.

4. Bake 60 to 65 minutes or until toothpick inserted near center comes out clean. Cool cake in pan 10 minutes; invert onto wire rack; cool completely.

5. Place remaining ¼ cup white chocolate chips in small microwavable bowl; microwave on HIGH 30 seconds. Stir; microwave on HIGH at 10-second intervals until melted and smooth. Drizzle over cake. Repeat with remaining ¼ cup butterscotch chips in another small microwavable bowl.

Makes 10 to 12 servings

CRANBERRY POUND CAKE

1½ **cups sugar**

1 **cup (2 sticks) butter, softened**

¼ **teaspoon salt**

¼ **teaspoon ground mace or nutmeg**

4 **eggs**

2 **cups cake flour***

1 **cup chopped fresh or thawed frozen cranberries**

*Or substitute 1¾ cups all-purpose flour and ¼ cup cornstarch; whisk until well blended.

1. Preheat oven to 350°F. Grease and flour 9×5-inch loaf pan.

2. Beat sugar, butter, salt and mace in large bowl with electric mixer at medium speed until light and fluffy. Beat in eggs, one at a time, until well blended. Add flour, ½ cup at a time, beating well at low speed after each addition. Fold in cranberries. Spoon batter into prepared pan.

3. Bake 60 to 70 minutes or until toothpick inserted into center comes out clean. Cool in pan on wire rack 5 minutes. Run knife around edges of pan to loosen cake; cool 30 minutes. Remove from pan; cool completely on wire rack.

Makes 1 loaf

MARBLED PUMPKIN CHEESECAKE

Crust

- 1 **cup gingersnap cookie crumbs**
- ½ **cup graham cracker crumbs**
- ¼ **cup sugar**
- 5 **tablespoons melted butter**

Cheesecake

- 4 **packages (8 ounces each) cream cheese, softened**
- ½ **cup sugar**
- 6 **eggs**
- 1 **cup sour cream**
- 1 **cup canned pumpkin**
- 2 **tablespoons all-purpose flour**
- 2 **teaspoons ground cinnamon**
- ½ **teaspoon ground ginger**
- ½ **teaspoon ground allspice**
- 3 **ounces semisweet chocolate, melted**

1. Preheat oven to 350°F. For crust, combine gingersnap cookie crumbs, graham cracker crumbs and ¼ cup sugar in small bowl. Stir in butter until well blended. Press onto bottom and 1 inch up side of 9-inch springform pan. Bake 8 minutes. Cool completely on wire rack.

2. *Increase oven temperature to 425°F.* Beat cream cheese in large bowl with electric mixer at medium-high speed about 3 minutes or until light and fluffy. Add ½ cup sugar; beat until well blended. Add eggs, one at a time, beating well after each addition. Add sour cream, pumpkin, flour, cinnamon, ginger and allspice; beat until well blended.

3. Pour 2 cups batter into small bowl; stir in melted chocolate until well blended. Pour remaining batter into prepared crust. Spoon chocolate batter in large swirls over pumpkin batter in crust; draw knife through mixture to marbleize.

4. Bake 15 minutes. *Reduce oven temperature to 300°F.* Bake 45 minutes (center of cheesecake will not be set). Turn off oven; let cheesecake stand in oven with door slightly ajar 1 hour. Cool to room temperature in pan on wire rack. Cover and refrigerate overnight.

5. Remove side of pan from cheesecake; place cheesecake on serving plate.

Makes 10 to 12 servings

CARROT CAKE

Cake

- 2 cups all-purpose flour
- 2 teaspoons baking soda
- 2 teaspoons ground cinnamon, plus additional for garnish
- 1 teaspoon salt
- 2 cups granulated sugar
- 1 cup vegetable oil
- 4 eggs
- 1 teaspoon vanilla
- 3 cups finely grated carrots (about 5 medium)
- 1 cup shredded coconut
- 1 can (8 ounces) crushed pineapple
- 1 cup chopped walnuts

Frosting

- 1 package (8 ounces) cream cheese, softened
- ½ cup (1 stick) butter, softened
- Pinch salt
- 1½ cups powdered sugar
- 1 to 2 tablespoons milk
- 1 teaspoon vanilla

1. Preheat oven to 350°F. Spray 13×9-inch baking pan with nonstick cooking spray.

2. Whisk flour, baking soda, 2 teaspoons cinnamon and 1 teaspoon salt in medium bowl until well blended. Beat granulated sugar and oil in large bowl until well blended. Add eggs, one at a time, beating until blended. Beat in 1 teaspoon vanilla. Add flour mixture; stir until blended. Add carrots, coconut, pineapple and walnuts; stir just until blended. Pour batter into prepared pan.

3. Bake 45 to 50 minutes or until toothpick inserted into center comes out clean. Cool completely in pan on wire rack.

4. For frosting, beat cream cheese, butter and pinch of salt in large bowl with electric mixer at medium speed about 3 minutes or until light and creamy. Add powdered sugar, 1 tablespoon milk and 1 teaspoon vanilla; beat at low speed until blended. Beat at medium speed 2 minutes or until frosting is smooth. Add

additional milk for softer frosting, if desired. Spread frosting over cake. Sprinkle with additional cinnamon, if desired.

Makes 12 servings

SPICED APPLE UPSIDE-DOWN CAKE

Cake

- ½ cup (1 stick) butter, melted
- ¾ cup packed dark brown sugar
- 2 medium tart apples, peeled and thinly sliced
- 1 package (about 15 ounces) carrot cake mix or spice cake mix, plus ingredients to prepare mix

Sauce

- ½ cup (1 stick) butter
- ½ cup packed dark brown sugar
- ¼ cup whiskey

1. Preheat oven to 350°F. Spray 9-inch springform pan with nonstick cooking spray. Wrap outside of pan tightly with foil.

2. For cake, pour melted butter into pan; tilt pan to spread butter evenly over bottom of pan. Sprinkle brown sugar evenly over butter. Arrange apple slices, overlapping slightly, in spiral pattern in pan.

3. Prepare cake mix according to package directions. Carefully spoon cake batter over apples.

4. Bake 1 hour or until toothpick inserted into center comes out clean. Immediately invert cake onto serving plate; let stand 5 minutes without removing pan. Remove side and bottom of pan; let cool completely.

5. For sauce, combine ½ cup butter and ½ cup brown sugar in small microwavable bowl; cover with plastic wrap. Microwave on HIGH 1 minute. Stir; microwave 30 seconds or until melted and well blended. Stir in whiskey.

6. Starting at outer edges of cake, spoon whiskey sauce over entire cake, allowing sauce to run down side.

Makes 8 servings

CARROT-SPICE BUTTERSCOTCH SQUARES

1½ **cups matchstick carrots**

¼ **cup water**

1 **package (about 15 ounces) spice cake mix**

1 **cup old-fashioned oats**

¾ **cup canola or vegetable oil**

2 **eggs**

¾ **cup butterscotch morsels**

½ **cup chopped pecans, toasted***

½ **cup flaked coconut**

*To toast pecans, spread on baking sheet. Bake in preheated 350°F oven 8 to 10 minutes or until golden brown, stirring frequently.

1. Preheat oven to 350°F. Spray 13×9-inch baking pan with nonstick cooking spray.

2. Place carrots and water in microwavable bowl; cover with plastic wrap and cut slit to vent. Microwave on HIGH 3 minutes or until tender; drain.

3. Beat cake mix, oats, oil and eggs in medium bowl with electric mixer at medium speed until blended. Stir in carrots. Spoon batter into prepared pan. Bake 23 minutes or until toothpick inserted into center comes out with moist crumbs.

4. Remove cake from oven; sprinkle evenly with butterscotch morsels, pecans and coconut. Press down toppings with rubber spatula. Cool completely in pan on wire rack. For best flavor, cover with foil and let stand overnight.

Makes 2 dozen squares

PUMPKIN SPICE CAKE

- 1½ cups canned pumpkin
- 1 cup buttermilk
- 2¾ cups all-purpose flour
- 1 tablespoon baking powder
- 1½ teaspoons baking soda
- 1½ teaspoons ground cinnamon
- ½ teaspoon salt
- ¼ teaspoon ground allspice
- ¼ teaspoon ground nutmeg
- ⅛ teaspoon ground ginger
- 1½ cups granulated sugar
- ¾ cup (1½ sticks) butter, softened
- 3 eggs

  Vanilla Maple Frosting (page 67)

1. Preheat oven to 350°F. Spray two (9-inch) round cake pans with nonstick cooking spray; dust with flour.

2. Combine pumpkin and buttermilk in medium bowl. Whisk flour, baking powder, baking soda, cinnamon, salt, allspice, nutmeg and ginger in another medium bowl until well blended.

3. Beat granulated sugar and butter in large bowl with electric mixer at medium speed 5 minutes or until light and fluffy. Add eggs, one at a time, beating well after each addition. With mixer running on low speed, alternately add flour mixture and pumpkin mixture, beating well after each addition. Pour batter into prepared pans.

4. Bake 30 to 40 minutes or until toothpick inserted into centers comes out clean. Cool in pans 10 minutes. Remove to wire racks; cool completely.

5. Prepare Vanilla Maple Frosting. Place one cake layer on serving plate; top with some of frosting. Spread remaining frosting over top and side of cake.

Makes 8 to 10 servings

VANILLA MAPLE FROSTING

- **1 cup (2 sticks) butter, softened**
- **1 teaspoon vanilla**
- **½ teaspoon maple flavoring**
- **4 cups powdered sugart**

1. Beat butter in large bowl with electric mixer at medium speed until light and fluffy. Add vanilla and maple flavoring; mix until well blended.

2. Gradually add powdered sugar; beat at medium-high speed about 5 minutes or until light and fluffy.

SWEET POTATO DUMP CAKE

1   **can (29 ounces) sweet potatoes in light syrup, drained**

1   **package (about 15 ounces) yellow cake mix**

3   **eggs**

1½   **teaspoons apple pie spice, plus additional for top of cake**

⅔   **cup chopped nuts, divided**

1. Preheat oven to 350°F. Spray 13×9-inch baking pan with nonstick cooking spray.

2. Place sweet potatoes in large bowl; mash with fork. Add cake mix, eggs and 1½ teaspoons apple pie spice; whisk 1 to 2 minutes or until well blended. Stir in ⅓ cup nuts. Spread batter in prepared pan; sprinkle with remaining ⅓ cup nuts and additional apple pie spice.

3. Bake 30 to 35 minutes or until toothpick inserted into center comes out clean. Cool in pan at least 15 minutes before serving.

Makes 12 to 16 servings

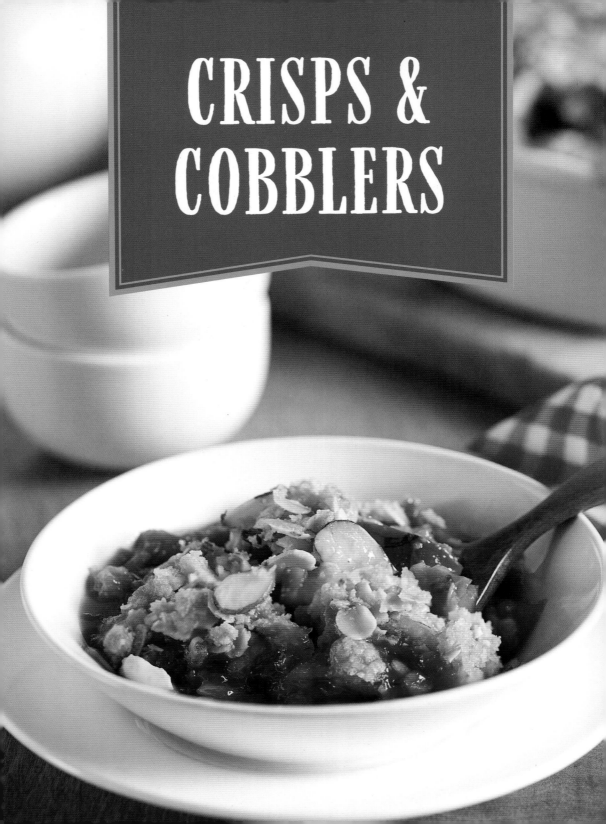

CRISPS & COBBLERS

PLUM RHUBARB CRUMBLE

1½ **pounds plums, each pitted and cut into 8 wedges (4 cups)**

1½ **pounds rhubarb, cut into ½-inch pieces (5 cups)**

1 **cup granulated sugar**

1 **teaspoon grated fresh ginger**

¼ **teaspoon ground nutmeg**

3 **tablespoons cornstarch**

¾ **cup old-fashioned oats**

½ **cup all-purpose flour**

½ **cup packed brown sugar**

½ **cup sliced almonds, toasted***

¼ **teaspoon salt**

½ **cup (1 stick) cold butter, cut into small pieces**

*To toast almonds, spread in single layer on ungreased baking sheet. Bake in preheated 350°F oven 5 minutes or until golden brown, stirring frequently.

1. Combine plums, rhubarb, granulated sugar, ginger and nutmeg in large bowl; toss to coat. Cover and let stand at room temperature 2 hours.

2. Preheat oven to 375°F. Spray 9-inch round or square baking dish with nonstick cooking spray. Line baking sheet with foil.

3. Pour juices from fruit mixture into small saucepan; bring to a boil over medium-high heat. Cook about 12 minutes or until reduced to syrupy consistency, stirring occasionally.** Stir in cornstarch until well blended. Stir mixture into bowl with fruit; pour into prepared baking dish.

4. Combine oats, flour, brown sugar, almonds and salt in medium bowl; mix well. Add butter; squeeze and rub into flour mixture using fingers until mixture is clumpy. Place baking dish on prepared baking sheet.

5. Bake 50 minutes or until filling is bubbly and topping is golden brown. Cool 1 hour before serving.

**If fruit is not juicy after 2 hours, liquid will take less time to reduce and will require less cornstarch to thicken.

Makes 6 to 8 servings

71

PEACH-CRANBERRY COBBLER WITH CORN BREAD BISCUITS

1 package (16 ounces) frozen sliced peaches, thawed

1 cup fresh or frozen cranberries or raspberries

⅓ cup orange juice

¼ cup packed brown sugar

⅓ cup plus 2 tablespoons all-purpose flour, divided

⅛ teaspoon ground allspice

3 tablespoons yellow cornmeal

1 tablespoon granulated sugar

1 teaspoon baking powder

¼ teaspoon salt

2 tablespoons cold butter, cut into small pieces

1 egg

3 tablespoons milk

1. Preheat oven to 400°F.

2. Combine peaches, cranberries and orange juice in large bowl; mix well. Combine brown sugar, 2 tablespoons flour and allspice in small bowl. Add to peach mixture; toss to coat. Spoon into 8-inch square baking dish.

3. Combine remaining ⅓ cup flour, cornmeal, granulated sugar, baking powder and salt in medium bowl; mix well. Cut in butter with pastry blender or two knives until mixture resembles coarse crumbs. Whisk egg and milk in small bowl; stir into flour mixture with fork just until moistened. Spoon topping evenly over fruit mixture.

4. Bake 30 to 35 minutes or until toothpick inserted into topping comes out clean.

Makes 6 servings

CINNAMON PEAR CRISP

8 pears, peeled and sliced

¾ cup unsweetened apple juice concentrate

½ cup golden raisins

¼ cup plus 3 tablespoons all-purpose flour, divided

1 teaspoon ground cinnamon

⅓ cup quick oats

3 tablespoons packed dark brown sugar

3 tablespoons butter, melted

1. Preheat oven to 375°F. Spray 11×7-inch baking dish with nonstick cooking spray.

2. Combine pears, apple juice concentrate, raisins, 3 tablespoons flour and cinnamon in large bowl; mix well. Transfer to prepared baking dish.

3. Combine oats, remaining ¼ cup flour, brown sugar and butter in medium bowl; stir until mixture resembles coarse crumbs. Sprinkle evenly over pear mixture.

4. Bake 1 hour or until topping is golden brown.

Makes 12 servings

TANGY CRANBERRY COBBLER

2 cups thawed frozen or fresh cranberries

1 cup dried cranberries

1 cup raisins

½ cup orange juice

¼ cup plus 2 tablespoons sugar, divided

2 teaspoons cornstarch

1 cup all-purpose flour

2 teaspoons baking powder

1 teaspoon ground cinnamon

¼ teaspoon salt

¼ cup (½ stick) cold butter, cut into small pieces

½ cup milk

1. Preheat oven to 400°F.

2. Combine cranberries, dried cranberries, raisins, orange juice, ¼ cup sugar and cornstarch in 9-inch square baking dish; toss to coat.

3. Combine flour, remaining 2 tablespoons sugar, baking powder, cinnamon and salt in large bowl; mix well. Cut in butter with pastry blender or electric mixer at low speed until mixture resembles coarse crumbs. Add milk; stir just until moistened. Drop batter by large spoonfuls over cranberry mixture.

4. Bake 35 to 40 minutes or until topping is light golden brown. Serve warm.

Makes 6 servings

SWEET POTATO AND APPLE COBBLER

1 cup all-purpose flour

¾ cup (1½ sticks) butter, melted, divided

¾ cup packed brown sugar, divided

¾ teaspoon salt, divided

¾ teaspoon ground cinnamon, divided

¼ teaspoon ground nutmeg or mace

¼ teaspoon ground cardamom

2 pounds sweet potatoes, peeled, halved lengthwise and thinly sliced

2 Granny Smith apples, peeled, and thinly sliced

1. Preheat oven to 375°F. Spray 2-quart baking dish with nonstick cooking spray.

2. Combine flour, ½ cup butter, ½ cup brown sugar, ½ teaspoon salt, ½ teaspoon cinnamon, nutmeg and cardamom in medium bowl until well blended.

3. Combine sweet potatoes, apples, remaining ¼ cup brown sugar, ¼ teaspoon salt and ¼ teaspoon cinnamon in medium bowl; mix well. Arrange mixture in prepared baking dish. Drizzle with remaining ¼ cup butter; season lightly with additional salt. Crumble topping over sweet potatoes and apples.

4. Bake 35 to 40 minutes or until topping is brown and potatoes and apples are tender.

Makes 9 servings

CINNAMON PLUM WALNUT COBBLER

¾ cup all-purpose flour

½ cup chopped walnuts

½ cup plus 3 tablespoons granulated sugar, divided

⅛ teaspoon salt

6 tablespoons (¾ stick) cold butter, cut into small pieces

4 to 5 tablespoons milk, divided

8 red plums (about 2½ pounds), cut into ¼-inch slices

2½ tablespoons cornstarch

¾ teaspoon ground cinnamon, divided

½ cup mascarpone cheese

2 tablespoons powdered sugar

1. Preheat oven to 350°F. Spray 8-inch square baking dish with nonstick cooking spray.

2. Combine flour, walnuts, 1 tablespoon granulated sugar and salt in food processor. Add butter; pulse until mixture resembles coarse crumbs. With motor running, add 1 to 2 tablespoons milk through feed tube just until soft dough forms. Wrap with plastic wrap; refrigerate 30 minutes.

3. Combine plums, ½ cup granulated sugar, cornstarch and ½ teaspoon cinnamon in large bowl; toss to coat. Spread fruit mixture evenly in prepared baking dish.

4. Bake 30 minutes. Meanwhile, roll out dough into 8-inch square. Cut out nine circles with 2¼-inch round cookie cutter. Remove scraps of dough; crumble over baked fruit or discard. Arrange dough circles over fruit; brush lightly with 1 tablespoon milk. Combine remaining 2 tablespoons sugar and ¼ teaspoon cinnamon in small bowl; sprinkle over dough.

5. Bake 30 to 35 minutes or until topping is golden brown. Meanwhile, combine mascarpone, powdered sugar and 2 tablespoons milk in small bowl; whisk until smooth. Serve with warm cobbler.

Makes 9 servings

APPLE BLACKBERRY CRISP

4 cups sliced peeled apples

Juice of ½ lemon

2 tablespoons granulated sugar

2 tablespoons Irish cream liqueur (optional)

1 teaspoon ground cinnamon, divided

1 cup old-fashioned oats

6 tablespoons (¾ stick) cold butter, cut into small pieces

⅔ cup packed brown sugar

¼ cup all-purpose flour

1 cup fresh blackberries

1. Preheat oven to 375°F. Grease 9-inch oval or 8-inch square baking dish.

2. Place apples in large bowl; drizzle with lemon juice. Add granulated sugar, liqueur, if desired, and ½ teaspoon cinnamon; toss to coat.

3. Combine oats, butter, brown sugar, flour and remaining ½ teaspoon cinnamon in food processor; pulse until combined, leaving some large pieces.

4. Gently stir blackberries into apple mixture. Spoon into prepared baking dish; sprinkle with oat mixture.

5. Bake 30 to 40 minutes or until filling is bubbly and topping is golden brown.

Makes 6 servings

VARIATION: This crisp can also be made without the blackberries; just add an additional 1 cup sliced apples.

PEAR AND CRANBERRY COBBLER

Filling

- **4 cups diced peeled ripe pears (3 to 4 medium)**
- **2 cups fresh cranberries**
- **½ cup sugar**
- **3 tablespoons all-purpose flour**
- **¼ teaspoon salt**
- **¼ teaspoon ground cinnamon**
- **2 tablespoons butter, cut into small pieces**

Biscuit Topping

- **1 cup all-purpose flour**
- **2 tablespoons sugar**
- **2 teaspoons baking powder**
- **¼ teaspoon salt**
- **¼ cup (½ stick) cold butter, cut into small pieces**
- **½ cup milk**

1. Preheat oven to 375°F. Spray 10-inch round or oval baking dish with nonstick cooking spray.

2. For filling, combine pears, cranberries, ½ cup sugar, 3 tablespoons flour, ¼ teaspoon salt and cinnamon in large bowl; toss to coat. Spoon into prepared baking dish; dot with 2 tablespoons butter.

3. For topping, combine 1 cup flour, 2 tablespoons sugar, baking powder and ¼ teaspoon salt in medium bowl; mix well. Cut in ¼ cup cold butter with pastry blender or electric mixer on low speed until mixture resembles coarse crumbs. Stir in milk to form soft sticky dough. Drop dough by tablespoonfuls over fruit mixture. Place baking dish on baking sheet.

4. Bake 25 to 35 minutes or until filling is bubbly and topping is golden brown. Serve warm.

Makes 6 to 8 servings

BUTTERMILK BISCUIT TOPPED DOUBLE PLUM COBBLER

Filling

- **10 red or black plums (about 2½ pounds), pitted and cut into ½-inch wedges**
- **⅔ cup plum preserves**
- **⅓ cup sugar**
- **2 tablespoons cornstarch**
- **¼ teaspoon salt**
- **¼ teaspoon almond extract**

Biscuits

- **1 cup all-purpose flour**
- **2 tablespoons plus 2 teaspoons sugar, divided**
- **1 teaspoon baking powder**
- **¼ teaspoon baking soda**
- **½ teaspoon salt**
- **5 tablespoons cold butter, cut into small pieces**
- **½ cup plus 2 tablespoons buttermilk, divided**

1. Preheat oven to 375°F. Spray 2-quart oval baking dish with nonstick cooking spray.

2. Combine plums, preserves, ⅓ cup sugar, cornstarch, ¼ teaspoon salt and almond extract in medium bowl; toss to coat. Spoon into prepared baking dish. Bake 20 minutes.

3. Meanwhile, combine flour, 2 tablespoons sugar, baking powder, baking soda and ½ teaspoon salt in medium bowl; mix well. Cut in butter with pastry blender or electric mixer on low speed until mixture resembles coarse crumbs. Add ½ cup buttermilk; stir just until moistened. Knead dough one or two times in bowl until it holds together. Shape dough into a disc. Wrap with plastic wrap; refrigerate 15 minutes.

4. Roll out dough to scant ½-inch thickness on floured surface. Cut out about 15 biscuits with 2-inch round biscuit cutter, pressing dough scraps together and rerolling if necessary. Arrange biscuits over warm plum mixture. Brush tops

of biscuits with remaining 2 tablespoons buttermilk; sprinkle with remaining
2 teaspoons sugar.

5. Bake about 30 minutes or until biscuits are lightly browned. Cover loosely
with foil; bake 10 minutes or until filling is thick and bubbly. Let stand 30 minutes
before serving.

Makes 8 servings

APPLE CRANBERRY CRUMBLE

4 **large apples (about 1⅓ pounds), peeled and cut into ¼-inch slices**

2 **cups fresh or frozen cranberries**

⅓ **cup granulated sugar**

6 **tablespoons all-purpose flour, divided**

1 **teaspoon apple pie spice, divided**

¼ **teaspoon salt, divided**

½ **cup chopped walnuts**

¼ **cup old-fashioned oats**

2 **tablespoons packed brown sugar**

¼ **cup (½ stick) cold butter, cut into small pieces**

1. Preheat oven to 375°F.

2. Combine apples, cranberries, granulated sugar, 2 tablespoons flour, ½ teaspoon apple pie spice and ⅛ teaspoon salt in large bowl; toss to coat. Spoon into medium (8-inch) cast iron skillet.

3. Combine remaining 4 tablespoons flour, walnuts, oats, brown sugar, remaining ½ teaspoon apple pie spice and ⅛ teaspoon salt in medium bowl; mix well. Cut in butter with pastry blender until mixture resembles coarse crumbs. Sprinkle over fruit mixture in skillet.

4. Bake 50 to 60 minutes or until filling is bubbly and topping is lightly browned.

Makes 4 servings

GINGER PEAR COBBLER

7 firm ripe pears (about 3½ pounds), peeled and cut into ½-inch pieces

⅓ cup packed brown sugar

1 cup plus 2 tablespoons all-purpose flour, divided

2 tablespoons lemon juice

2 teaspoons ground ginger, divided

½ teaspoon ground cinnamon

⅛ teaspoon ground nutmeg

¼ cup granulated sugar

1½ teaspoons baking powder

¼ teaspoon salt

¼ cup (½ stick) cold butter, cut into small pieces

¼ cup whipping cream

1 egg, lightly beaten

Sparkling or coarse sugar (optional)

1. Preheat oven to 375°F. Spray 9-inch square baking dish with nonstick cooking spray.

2. Combine pears, brown sugar, 2 tablespoons flour, lemon juice, 1 teaspoon ginger, cinnamon and nutmeg in large bowl; toss to coat. Spoon into prepared baking dish.

3. Combine remaining 1 cup flour, 1 teaspoon ginger, granulated sugar, baking powder and salt in medium bowl; mix well. Add butter; mix with fingertips until shaggy clumps form. Add cream and egg; stir just until combined. Drop topping, 2 tablespoonfuls at a time, into mounds over pear mixture. Sprinkle with sparkling sugar, if desired.

4. Bake 40 to 45 minutes or until filling is bubbly and topping is golden brown.

Makes 8 to 10 servings

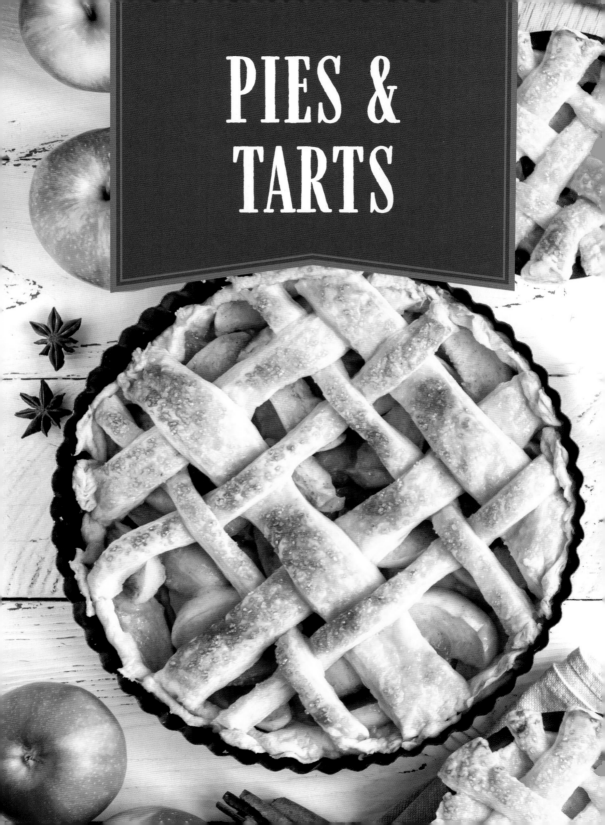

PIES & TARTS

CLASSIC APPLE PIE

Double-Crust Pie Pastry (page 115)

5 **Granny Smith apples, peeled and cut into ½-inch wedges (about 3 pounds)**

½ **cup granulated sugar**

¼ **cup packed brown sugar**

1 **tablespoon cornstarch**

2 **teaspoons lemon juice**

2 **teaspoons ground cinnamon**

½ **teaspoon vanilla**

¼ **teaspoon salt**

⅛ **teaspoon ground nutmeg**

⅛ **teaspoon ground allspice**

1 **tablespoon whipping cream**

1. Prepare pie pastry. Roll out half of pastry into 11-inch circle on lightly floured surface. Press into 9-inch pie plate; trim edge.

2. Combine apples, granulated sugar, brown sugar, cornstarch, lemon juice, cinnamon, vanilla, salt, nutmeg and allspice in large bowl; toss to coat. Let stand 30 minutes.

3. Preheat oven to 350°F. Roll out second crust into 10-inch circle; cut into strips. Pour filling into crust. Arrange pastry strips in lattice design over fruit. Tuck ends of strips under edge of bottom crust; seal edge and crimp or flute. Brush pastry with cream.

4. Bake 1 hour or until apples are very soft when pierced with knife. If top pastry is browning too quickly, cover with foil. Cool completely on wire rack.

Makes 8 servings

RUSTIC CRANBERRY-PEAR GALETTE

¼ cup sugar, divided

1 tablespoon plus 1 teaspoon cornstarch

2 teaspoons ground cinnamon or apple pie spice

4 cups thinly sliced peeled Bartlett pears

¼ cup dried cranberries

1 teaspoon vanilla

¼ teaspoon almond extract (optional)

⅛ teaspoon salt

1 refrigerated pie crust, at room temperature (half of 15-ounce package)

1 egg white

1 tablespoon water

1. Preheat oven to 450°F. Line baking sheet or pizza pan with parchment paper or spray with nonstick cooking spray.

2. Reserve 1 teaspoon sugar. Combine remaining sugar, cornstarch and cinnamon in medium bowl; mix well. Add pears, cranberries, vanilla, almond extract, if desired, and salt; toss to coat.

3. Place crust on prepared pan. Spoon pear mixture into center of crust, leaving 2-inch border. Fold edge of crust 2 inches over pear mixture, overlapping and pleating as necessary.

4. Whisk egg white and water in small bowl until well blended. Brush over crust; sprinkle with reserved 1 teaspoon sugar.

5. Bake 25 minutes or until pears are tender and crust is golden brown.* Cool on baking sheet on wire rack 30 minutes. Serve warm.

*If edge browns too quickly, cover loosely with foil after 15 minutes of baking.

Makes 8 servings

SWEET POTATO PECAN PIE

1 large sweet potato (about 1 pound)

3 eggs, divided

8 tablespoons granulated sugar, divided

8 tablespoons packed brown sugar, divided

2 tablespoons butter, melted, divided

½ teaspoon ground cinnamon

½ teaspoon salt, divided

1 frozen 9-inch deep-dish pie crust

½ cup dark corn syrup

1½ teaspoons lemon juice

1½ teaspoons vanilla

1 cup pecan halves

Vanilla ice cream (optional)

1. Preheat oven to 350°F. Prick sweet potato all over with fork. Bake 1 hour or until fork-tender; let stand until cool enough to handle. *Reduce oven temperature to 300°F.*

2. Peel sweet potato and place in large bowl of stand mixer. Add 1 egg, 2 tablespoons granulated sugar, 2 tablespoons brown sugar, 1 tablespoon butter, cinnamon and ¼ teaspoon salt; beat at medium speed 5 minutes or until smooth and fluffy. Spread mixture in frozen crust; place in refrigerator.

3. Combine corn syrup, remaining 6 tablespoons granulated sugar, 6 tablespoons brown sugar, 1 tablespoon butter, lemon juice, vanilla and remaining ¼ teaspoon salt in clean mixer bowl; beat at medium speed 5 minutes. Add remaining 2 eggs; beat 5 minutes. Place crust on baking sheet. Spread pecans over sweet potato filling; pour corn syrup mixture evenly over pecans.

4. Bake 1 hour or until center is set and top is deep golden brown. Cool completely. Serve with ice cream, if desired.

Makes 8 servings

SOUR CREAM SQUASH PIE

1 package (12 ounces) frozen winter squash, thawed and drained

½ cup sour cream

¼ cup sugar

1 egg

1½ teaspoons pumpkin pie spice

½ teaspoon salt

½ teaspoon vanilla

¾ cup evaporated milk

1 (9-inch) graham cracker pie crust

¼ cup chopped hazelnuts, toasted (optional)*

*To toast hazelnuts, spread on baking sheet. Bake in preheated 350°F oven 8 to 10 minutes or until golden brown, stirring frequently.

1. Preheat oven to 350°F.

2. Whisk squash, sour cream, sugar, egg, pumpkin pie spice, salt and vanilla in large bowl until blended. Whisk in evaporated milk until blended. Pour into crust.

3. Bake 1 hour and 10 minutes or until set. Cool completely on wire rack. Sprinkle with hazelnuts just before serving, if desired.

Makes 8 servings

VEGETABLE TART

Pastry Dough

- **1** teaspoon active dry yeast
- **⅓** cup warm water (115°F)
- **1** egg
- **3** tablespoons sour cream
- **1¼** cups all-purpose flour
- **¼** cup whole wheat flour
- **¼** teaspoon salt

Filling

- **1** small sweet potato, peeled and cut crosswise into ¼-inch slices
- **2** tablespoons olive or vegetable oil, divided
- **1** cup sliced mushrooms
- **1** medium zucchini, sliced
- **1** parsnip or carrot, sliced
- **1** medium red bell pepper, cut into 1-inch pieces
- **½** cup thinly sliced leeks
- **8** cloves garlic, minced
- **1** teaspoon dried basil
- **½** teaspoon dried rosemary
- **½** teaspoon salt
- Black pepper
- **¼** cup grated Parmesan cheese
- **1** egg, beaten

1. For pastry dough, sprinkle yeast over warm water in medium bowl; stir until yeast is dissolved. Let stand 5 minutes or until mixture is bubbly. Add egg and sour cream; mix until smooth. Stir in flours and ¼ teaspoon salt to make soft dough. Knead dough on lightly floured surface 1 to 2 minutes or until smooth. Shape dough into a ball. Place in large lightly greased bowl; turn to grease top. Cover and let rest in warm place 20 minutes.

2. Preheat oven to 400°F. Spray baking sheet with nonstick cooking spray. Place sweet potato on prepared baking sheet; drizzle with 1 tablespoon oil. Toss to coat; arrange in single layer. Bake 15 to 20 minutes or until tender, turning once.

3. Heat remaining 1 tablespoon oil in large skillet over medium heat. Add mushrooms, zucchini, parsnip, bell pepper, leeks, garlic, basil and rosemary; cook and stir 8 to 10 minutes or until vegetables are tender. Season with ½ teaspoon salt and black pepper.

4. Roll out dough into 14-inch round on lightly floured surface; place on baking sheet or large pizza pan. Arrange sweet potato slices evenly over crust, leaving 2½-inch border. Spoon vegetable mixture evenly over potatoes; sprinkle with cheese. Fold edge of dough over edge of vegetable mixture, pleating dough as necessary, to fit. Brush edge of dough with egg.

5. Bake 25 minutes or until golden brown. Cut into wedges; serve warm.

Makes 8 servings

APPLE CRUNCH PIE

- 1 refrigerated pie crust (half of 15-ounce package)
- ¾ cup all-purpose flour, divided
- ¼ cup packed brown sugar
- ¼ cup chopped walnuts
- 4 tablespoons (½ stick) butter, melted, divided
- 1¼ teaspoons ground cinnamon, divided
- ¾ teaspoon ground nutmeg, divided
- 1 cup granulated sugar
- ½ teaspoon ground ginger
- ¼ teaspoon salt
- 4 cups diced peeled apples

1. Preheat oven to 350°F. Place pie crust in 9-inch pie plate; flute edge as desired.

2. Combine ½ cup flour, brown sugar, walnuts, 2 tablespoons butter, ¼ teaspoon cinnamon and ¼ teaspoon nutmeg in small bowl; mix well. Spread in single layer on baking sheet. Bake 20 minutes on bottom rack of oven.

3. Combine remaining ¼ cup flour, granulated sugar, remaining 2 tablespoons butter, 1 teaspoon cinnamon, ½ teaspoon nutmeg, ginger and salt in large bowl; mix well. Add apples; toss to coat. Place apple mixture in prepared crust. Bake 20 minutes on top rack of oven.

4. Remove baking sheet from oven. Let stand 5 minutes or until cool enough to handle; crumble into topping and sprinkle over apple mixture.

5. Bake 25 to 35 minutes or until apples are tender.

Makes 8 servings

GINGER PLUM TART

1 refrigerated pie crust (half of 15-ounce package)

1¾ pounds plums, cut into ½-inch slices

½ cup plus 1 teaspoon sugar, divided

1½ tablespoons all-purpose flour

1½ teaspoons ground ginger

¼ teaspoon ground cinnamon

⅛ teaspoon salt

1 egg

2 teaspoons water

1. Preheat oven to 400°F. Let pie crust stand at room temperature 10 minutes. Combine plums, ½ cup sugar, flour, ginger, cinnamon and salt in large bowl; toss to coat.

2. Roll out crust on lightly floured surface into 14-inch circle. Transfer crust to large (10-inch) ungreased cast iron skillet. Mound plum mixture in center of crust, leaving 2-inch border around fruit. Fold crust up over filling, pleating as necessary and gently pressing crust into fruit to secure.

3. Beat egg and water in small bowl; brush over crust. Sprinkle with remaining 1 teaspoon sugar.

4. Bake about 45 minutes or until crust is golden brown.

Makes 8 servings

PUMPKIN PIE

1 package (15 ounces) refrigerated pie crusts (2 crusts), divided

1 can (15 ounces) pumpkin

1¼ cups half-and-half, divided

3 eggs

⅔ cup plus 2 tablespoons sugar, divided

¼ cup honey

2 teaspoons ground cinnamon

1 teaspoon ground allspice

1 teaspoon ground nutmeg

½ teaspoon ground ginger

½ teaspoon ground cloves

½ teaspoon salt

1. Preheat oven to 425°F.

2. Reserve one pie crust for decorations. Roll out remaining pie crust into 10-inch circle on lightly floured surface. Press into 9-inch pie plate; trim edge and flute.

3. Combine pumpkin, 1 cup half-and-half, eggs, ⅔ cup sugar, honey, cinnamon, allspice, nutmeg, ginger, cloves and salt in large bowl; mix well. Pour into crust.

4. Bake 10 minutes. *Reduce oven temperature to 350°F.* Bake 40 to 45 minutes or until crust is golden brown and knife inserted into center comes out clean. Cool completely on wire rack.

5. For decorations, *increase oven temperature to 400°F.* Roll out reserved pie crust to ⅛-inch thickness on lightly floured surface. Cut out leaf shapes with cookie cutters; place 1 inch apart on ungreased baking sheet. Brush leaves with remaining ¼ cup half-and-half; sprinkle with remaining 2 tablespoons sugar. Bake 10 to 15 minutes or until golden brown. Remove to wire rack; cool completely.

6. Arrange leaves on pie just before serving.

Makes 8 to 10 servings

APPLE PIE WITH CHEDDAR

Single-Crust Pie Pastry (page 109)

Streusel

- ⅓ cup all-purpose flour
- ⅓ cup granulated sugar
- ⅓ cup packed brown sugar
- ¼ teaspoon salt
- 5 tablespoons cold butter, cut into small pieces

Filling

- 8 cups sliced peeled tart apples
- ½ cup packed dark brown sugar
- ⅓ cup granulated sugar
- 3 tablespoons all-purpose flour
- ½ teaspoon ground cinnamon
- ¼ teaspoon salt
- 1 cup (4 ounces) shredded sharp Cheddar cheese, divided

1. Prepare pie pastry. For streusel, combine ⅓ cup flour, ⅓ cup granulated sugar, ⅓ cup brown sugar and ¼ teaspoon salt in medium bowl. Cut in butter with pastry blender or blend with fingers until mixture resembles coarse crumbs.

2. Preheat oven to 425°F. Combine apples, ½ cup brown sugar, ⅓ cup granulated sugar, 3 tablespoons flour, cinnamon and ¼ teaspoon salt in large bowl; toss to coat.

3. Roll out pastry into 11-inch circle on floured surface. Sprinkle with ½ cup cheese; roll lightly to adhere. Line 9-inch pie plate with pastry; flute edge.

4. Spoon filling into crust, packing down. Sprinkle with streusel. Place pie on baking sheet.

5. Bake 15 minutes. *Reduce oven temperature to 350°F.* Loosely tent pie with foil; bake 35 minutes. Remove foil; sprinkle pie with remaining ½ cup cheese. Bake 10 minutes or until cheese is melted and crust is golden brown. Cool at least 30 minutes before slicing.

Makes 8 servings

SINGLE-CRUST PIE PASTRY

- 1¼ **cups all-purpose flour**
- ½ **teaspoon salt**
- 6 **tablespoons cold butter, cut into pieces**
- 3 **to 4 tablespoons ice water**
- 1½ **teaspoons cider vinegar**

Combine flour and salt in medium bowl. Cut in butter with pastry blender or stand mixer on low speed until mixture resembles coarse crumbs. Combine 3 tablespoons ice water and vinegar in small bowl. Sprinkle over flour mixture, mixing with fork until dough forms. Add additional water as needed. Shape dough into a disc; wrap in plastic wrap. Refrigerate at least 30 minutes.

Makes pastry for one 9-inch pie

BOURBON-LACED SWEET POTATO PIE

1 pound sweet potatoes, peeled and cut into 1-inch chunks (about 2 medium)

2 tablespoons butter

¾ cup packed brown sugar

1 teaspoon ground cinnamon

¼ teaspoon salt

2 eggs

¾ cup whipping cream

¼ cup bourbon or whiskey

1 refrigerated pie crust (half of 15-ounce package)

Sweetened Whipped Cream (recipe follows, optional)

1. Preheat oven to 350°F. Place sweet potatoes in large saucepan; cover with water. Bring to a boil over high heat. Reduce heat to low; simmer 20 minutes or until very tender. Drain; transfer to large bowl.

2. Add butter, brown sugar, cinnamon and salt; beat with electric mixer at medium speed until smooth. Add eggs, one at a time, beating well after each addition. Beat in cream and bourbon.

3. Line 9-inch pie plate with crust; flute edges. Pour filling into crust. Bake 50 minutes or until knife inserted near center comes out clean. Transfer to wire rack; cool at least 1 hour before serving.

4. Prepare sweetened whipped cream, if desired; serve with pie.

Makes 8 servings

TIP: The pie can be cooled completely, covered and chilled up to 24 hours before serving. Let stand it at room temperature at least 30 minutes before serving.

SWEETENED WHIPPED CREAM: Combine 1 cup cold whipping cream, 2 tablespoons powdered sugar and ½ teaspoon vanilla in large bowl; whip with electric mixer at high speed or whisk until soft peaks form. *Do not overbeat.* Refrigerate until ready to serve.

SOUR CREAM APPLE TART

5 tablespoons butter, divided

¾ cup graham cracker crumbs

1¼ teaspoons ground cinnamon, divided

1⅓ cups sour cream

¾ cup sugar, divided

½ cup all-purpose flour, divided

2 eggs

1 teaspoon vanilla

5 cups coarsely chopped peeled Jonathan apples or other tart apples

1. Preheat oven to 350°F.

2. Melt 3 tablespoons butter in small saucepan over medium heat. Stir in graham cracker crumbs and ¼ teaspoon cinnamon until well blended. Press crumb mixture firmly onto bottom of 9-inch springform pan. Bake 10 minutes. Remove to wire rack to cool.

3. Beat sour cream, ½ cup sugar and 2 tablespoons flour in large bowl with electric mixer at medium speed until well blended. Beat in eggs and vanilla until well blended. Stir in apples. Spoon into prepared crust.

4. Bake 35 minutes or just until center is set.

5. Preheat broiler. Combine remaining 1 teaspoon cinnamon, ¼ cup sugar and 6 tablespoons flour in small bowl. Cut in remaining 2 tablespoons butter with pastry blender or blend with fingers until mixture resembles coarse crumbs. Sprinkle over top of pie.

6. Broil 3 to 4 minutes or until topping is golden brown. Let stand 15 minutes before serving.

Makes 10 servings

CRANBERRY APPLE NUT PIE

Double-Crust Pie Pastry (page 115)

1 cup sugar

3 tablespoons all-purpose flour

¼ teaspoon salt

4 cups sliced peeled tart apples (4 large apples)

2 cups fresh or frozen cranberries

½ cup golden raisins

½ cup chopped pecans

1 tablespoon grated lemon peel

2 tablespoons butter, cut into small pieces

1 egg, beaten

1. Prepare pie pastry. Preheat oven to 425°F. Roll out half of pastry into 11-inch circle on floured surface. Line 9-inch pie plate with pastry.

2. Combine sugar, flour and salt in large bowl. Stir in apples, cranberries, raisins, pecans and lemon peel; toss to coat. Pour into crust; dot with butter.

3. Roll out remaining pastry into 11-inch circle. Place over filling; trim excess dough. Seal and flute edge. Cut three slits in center of top crust. Lightly brush top crust with egg.

4. Bake 35 minutes or until apples are tender when pierced with fork and crust is golden brown. Cool on wire rack 15 minutes. Serve warm or cool completely.

Makes 8 servings

DOUBLE-CRUST PIE PASTRY

2 **cups all-purpose flour**

1 **tablespoon sugar**

½ **teaspoon salt**

¾ **cup (1½ sticks) cold butter, cut into pieces**

6 **to 8 tablespoons ice water**

1 **tablespoon cider vinegar**

Combine flour, sugar and salt in medium bowl. Cut in butter with pastry blender or electric mixer on low speed until mixture resembles coarse crumbs. Combine 6 tablespoons ice water and vinegar in small bowl. Sprinkle water mixture, 1 tablespoon at a time, over flour mixture, mixing with fork until dough forms. Add additional water, if necessary. Divide dough in half. Shape each half into a disc; wrap in plastic wrap. Refrigerate at least 30 minutes.

Makes pastry for one 9-inch pie

RUSTIC PLUM TART

¼ cup (½ stick) plus 1 tablespoon butter, divided

3 cups sliced plums (about 6 medium)

¼ cup granulated sugar

½ cup all-purpose flour

½ cup old-fashioned or quick oats

¼ cup packed brown sugar

½ teaspoon ground cinnamon

¼ teaspoon salt

1 refrigerated pie crust (half of 15-ounce package)

1 egg

1 teaspoon water

1 tablespoon chopped crystallized ginger

1. Preheat oven to 425°F. Line baking sheet with parchment paper.

2. Melt 1 tablespoon butter in large skillet over high heat. Add plums; cook and stir 3 minutes or until softened. Stir in granulated sugar; cook 1 minute or until juices are thickened. Remove from heat; set aside.

3. Combine flour, oats, brown sugar, cinnamon and salt in medium bowl. Cut in remaining ¼ cup butter with pastry blender or electric mixer on low speed until mixture resembles coarse crumbs.

4. Unroll pie crust on prepared baking sheet. Beat egg and water in small bowl; brush lightly over crust. Sprinkle with ¼ cup oat mixture, leaving 2-inch border around edge of crust. Spoon plums over oat mixture, leaving juices in skillet. Sprinkle with ginger. Fold crust edge up around plums, overlapping as necessary. Sprinkle with remaining oat mixture. Brush edge of crust with egg mixture.

5. Bake 25 minutes or until crust is golden brown. Cool slightly before serving.

Makes 8 servings

WARM APPLE CROSTATA

1¾ cups all-purpose flour

⅓ cup granulated sugar

½ teaspoon plus ⅛ teaspoon salt, divided

¾ cup (1½ sticks) cold butter, cut into small pieces

3 tablespoons ice water

2 teaspoons vanilla

6 to 8 Pink Lady or small Honeycrisp apples (about 1½ pounds), peeled and cut into ¼-inch slices

¼ cup packed brown sugar

1 tablespoon lemon juice

1 teaspoon ground cinnamon

⅛ teaspoon ground nutmeg

4 teaspoons butter, cut into very small pieces

1 egg, beaten

1 to 2 teaspoons turbinado sugar

Vanilla ice cream

Caramel sauce or ice cream topping

1. Combine flour, granulated sugar and ½ teaspoon salt in food processor; process 5 seconds. Add ¾ cup cold butter; process about 10 seconds or until mixture resembles coarse crumbs.

2. Combine ice water and vanilla in small bowl. With motor running, pour mixture through feed tube; process 12 seconds or until dough begins to come together. Shape dough into a disc; wrap in plastic wrap and refrigerate 30 minutes.

3. Meanwhile, combine apples, brown sugar, lemon juice, cinnamon, nutmeg and remaining ⅛ teaspoon salt in large bowl; toss to coat. Preheat oven to 400°F.

4. Line two baking sheets with parchment paper. Cut dough into four pieces; roll out each piece into 7-inch circle on floured surface. Place on prepared baking sheets; mound apples in center of dough circles (about 1 cup apples for each crostata). Fold or roll up edges of dough towards center to create rim of crostata. Dot apples with 4 teaspoons butter. Brush dough with egg; sprinkle dough and apples with turbinado sugar.

5. Bake about 20 minutes or until apples are tender and crust is golden brown. Serve warm topped with ice cream and caramel sauce.

Makes 4 tarts (4 to 8 servings)

CUPCAKES & MUFFINS

BAKED PUMPKIN BITES

¾ **cup canned pumpkin**

½ **cup packed brown sugar**

½ **cup milk**

⅓ **cup canola or vegetable oil**

1 **egg**

1 **teaspoon vanilla**

1¾ **cups all-purpose flour**

2 **teaspoons baking powder**

2 **teaspoons ground cinnamon, divided**

½ **teaspoon ground nutmeg**

½ **teaspoon salt**

1 **cup powdered sugar**

⅓ **cup maple syrup**

¼ **cup granulated sugar**

1. Preheat oven to 350°F. Spray 24 mini muffin cups with nonstick cooking spray.

2. Combine pumpkin, brown sugar, milk, oil, egg and vanilla in large bowl; stir until well blended. Add flour, baking powder, 1 teaspoon cinnamon, nutmeg and salt; stir just until combined. Scoop heaping tablespoonfuls of batter into prepared muffin cups.

3. Bake 12 minutes or until toothpick inserted into centers comes out clean. Cool in pans 5 minutes; remove to wire racks.

4. Combine powdered sugar and maple syrup in small bowl; microwave on HIGH 30 seconds. Stir until well blended and smooth. Dip tops of muffins into syrup mixture; return to wire racks to set. Combine granulated sugar and remaining 1 teaspoon cinnamon in small bowl; sprinkle over muffins.

Makes 24 mini muffins

LEMON-GLAZED ZUCCHINI MUFFINS

- 2 cups all-purpose flour
- ⅔ cup granulated sugar
- 1 tablespoon baking powder
- 2 teaspoons grated lemon peel
- 1 teaspoon salt
- ½ teaspoon ground nutmeg
- ½ cup chopped walnuts, pecans or hazelnuts
- ½ cup dried fruit bits or golden raisins
- ½ cup milk
- ⅓ cup canola or vegetable oil
- 2 eggs
- 1 cup packed shredded zucchini
- ¼ cup powdered sugar
- 1 to 1½ teaspoons fresh lemon juice

1. Preheat oven to 400°F. Line 12 standard (2½-inch) muffin cups with paper baking cups.

2. Combine flour, granulated sugar, baking powder, lemon peel, salt and nutmeg in large bowl; stir in nuts and fruit. Whisk milk, oil and eggs in medium bowl until blended. Pour into flour mixture; add zucchini. Stir just until dry ingredients are moistened. Spoon evenly into prepared muffin cups.

3. Bake 20 to 25 minutes or until toothpick inserted into centers comes out clean. Remove from pan; cool on wire rack. Meanwhile, combine powdered sugar and lemon juice in small bowl until smooth. Drizzle over warm muffins.

Makes 12 muffins

SWEET POTATO SPICE CUPCAKES

1¼ pounds sweet potatoes, peeled and quartered

1½ cups all-purpose flour

1¼ cups granulated sugar

2 teaspoons baking powder

1 teaspoon baking soda

1 teaspoon ground cinnamon

½ teaspoon salt

¼ teaspoon ground allspice

¾ cup canola or vegetable oil

2 eggs

½ cup chopped walnuts or pecans, plus additional for garnish

½ cup raisins

Cream Cheese Frosting (page 125)

1. Place sweet potatoes in large saucepan; add enough water to cover by 1 inch. Cover and cook over medium heat 30 minutes or until fork-tender, adding additional water if necessary. Drain sweet potatoes; place in medium bowl. Mash with fork or potato masher. Measure 2 cups.

2. Preheat oven to 325°F. Line 18 standard (2½-inch) muffin cups with paper baking cups.

3. Combine flour, granulated sugar, baking powder, baking soda, cinnamon, salt and allspice in medium bowl.

4. Stir 2 cups mashed sweet potatoes, oil and eggs in large bowl until blended. Add flour mixture; stir until well blended. Fold in ½ cup walnuts and raisins. Spoon evenly into prepared muffin cups.

5. Bake 25 to 30 minutes or until toothpick inserted into centers comes out clean. Cool completely in pans on wire racks.

6. Prepare Cream Cheese Frosting. Frost cupcakes. Top with additional walnuts, if desired.

Makes 18 cupcakes

CREAM CHEESE FROSTING: Beat 8 ounces softened cream cheese and ¼ cup (½ stick) softened butter in medium bowl with electric mixer at medium-high speed until creamy. Beat in ¼ teaspoon salt and ¼ teaspoon vanilla. Gradually beat in 1½ cups sifted powdered sugar until well blended. Beat in milk 1 tablespoon at a time if necessary for desired consistency. Makes about 3 cups.

PINEAPPLE ZUCCHINI CUPCAKES WITH SOUR CREAM FROSTING

Cupcakes

- 1 package (about 15 ounces) yellow cake mix without pudding in the mix
- 1 cup buttermilk
- 3 eggs
- 1/3 cup canola or vegetable oil
- 1 teaspoon ground cinnamon
- 1/2 teaspoon ground nutmeg
- 1/4 teaspoon ground allspice
- 2 cups grated zucchini (1 medium)
- 1 can (8 ounces) crushed pineapple, well drained

Frosting

- 4 cups powdered sugar
- 2/3 cup sour cream
- 1/4 cup (1/2 stick) butter, softened
- 2 teaspoons grated orange peel

  Candied orange peel (optional)

1. Preheat oven to 350°F. Line 24 standard (2½-inch) muffin cups with paper baking cups; spray paper cups with nonstick cooking spray.

2. Beat cake mix, buttermilk, eggs, oil, cinnamon, nutmeg and allspice in large bowl according to package directions. Stir in zucchini and pineapple. Spoon batter evenly into prepared muffin cups.

3. Bake 20 to 22 minutes or until toothpick inserted into centers comes out clean. Cool in pans 10 minutes. Remove to wire racks; cool completely.

4. Beat powdered sugar, sour cream and butter in large bowl with electric mixer at low speed. Beat at medium speed until smooth. Stir in 2 teaspoons orange peel. Frost cupcakes. Garnish with candied orange peel. Serve at room temperature. Refrigerate leftovers.

Makes 24 cupcakes

SPICED SWEET POTATO MUFFINS

⅓ cup plus 2 tablespoons packed brown sugar, divided

2 teaspoons ground cinnamon, divided

1½ cups all-purpose flour

2 teaspoons baking powder

½ teaspoon baking soda

½ teaspoon salt

½ teaspoon ground allspice

1 cup mashed cooked or canned sweet potatoes

¾ cup buttermilk

¼ cup canola or vegetable oil

1 egg

1. Preheat oven to 425°F. Spray 12 standard (2½-inch) muffin cups with nonstick cooking spray. Combine 2 tablespoons brown sugar and 1 teaspoon cinnamon in small bowl; mix well.

2. Combine flour, remaining ⅓ cup brown sugar, 1 teaspoon cinnamon, baking powder, baking soda, salt and allspice in large bowl. Combine sweet potatoes, buttermilk, oil and egg in medium bowl; mix well. Stir into flour mixture just until moistened. Spoon evenly into prepared muffin cups. Sprinkle with brown sugar-cinnamon mixture.

3. Bake 14 to 16 minutes or until toothpick inserted into centers comes out clean. Remove to wire rack; cool completely.

Makes 12 muffins

ZUCCHINI BASIL CUPCAKES

1¼ cups all-purpose flour

1½ teaspoons baking powder

1 teaspoon baking soda

½ teaspoon salt

1 cup granulated sugar

½ cup vegetable oil

2 eggs

½ cup milk

1 cup grated zucchini, squeezed to remove liquid

¼ cup finely chopped fresh basil

1 package (8 ounces) cream cheese, softened

¼ cup (½ stick) butter, softened

1¾ cups powdered sugar

1 teaspoon vanilla

Small whole fresh basil leaves (optional)

1. Preheat oven to 350°F. Line 16 standard (2½-inch) muffin cups with paper baking cups.

2. Combine flour, baking powder, baking soda and salt in small bowl. Whisk granulated sugar, oil and eggs in large bowl until well blended. Add flour mixture and milk; mix well. Stir in zucchini and chopped basil. Spoon batter evenly into prepared muffin cups.

3. Bake 25 minutes or until toothpick inserted into centers comes out clean. Cool cupcakes in pans 5 minutes. Remove to wire racks; cool completely.

4. Beat cream cheese and butter in large bowl with electric mixer at medium speed until well combined. Add powdered sugar and vanilla; beat at low speed 1 minute. Beat at medium-high speed 5 minutes or until fluffy. Frost cupcakes; garnish with basil leaves.

Makes 16 cupcakes

GINGER SQUASH MUFFINS

1½ **cups all-purpose flour**

⅓ **cup whole wheat flour**

⅓ **cup granulated sugar**

¼ **cup packed dark brown sugar**

2½ **teaspoons baking powder**

1 **teaspoon ground cinnamon**

½ **teaspoon baking soda**

½ **teaspoon salt**

½ **teaspoon ground ginger**

1 **cup frozen winter squash, thawed***

2 **eggs, beaten**

⅓ **cup canola or vegetable oil**

¼ **cup finely chopped walnuts**

2 **tablespoons finely chopped crystallized ginger**

*One 12-ounce package frozen squash yields about 1 cup squash. Or use puréed cooked fresh butternut squash.

1. Preheat oven to 375°F. Grease 12 standard (2½-inch) muffin cups.

2. Combine all-purpose flour, whole wheat flour, granulated sugar, brown sugar, baking powder, cinnamon, baking soda, salt and ground ginger in large bowl; mix well.

3. Combine squash, eggs and oil in small bowl until well blended. Add to flour mixture; stir just until dry ingredients are moistened. Stir in walnuts and crystallized ginger. Spoon batter evenly into prepared muffin cups.

4. Bake 18 to 20 minutes or until toothpick inserted into centers comes out clean. Cool in pan 5 minutes. Remove to wire rack; cool completely.

Makes 12 muffins

CARROT CREAM CHEESE CUPCAKES

1 package (8 ounces) cream cheese, softened

¼ cup powdered sugar

1 package (about 15 ounces) spice cake mix, plus ingredients to prepare mix

2 cups grated carrots

2 tablespoons finely chopped crystallized ginger

1 container (16 ounces) cream cheese frosting

3 tablespoons maple syrup

Orange peel strips (optional)

1. Preheat oven to 350°F. Spray 14 jumbo (3½-inch) muffin cups with nonstick cooking spray or line with paper baking cups.

2. Beat cream cheese and powdered sugar in medium bowl with electric mixer at medium speed 1 minute or until light and fluffy. Cover and refrigerate until ready to use.

3. Prepare cake mix according to package directions; stir in carrots and ginger. Spoon batter into prepared muffin cups, filling one third full (about ¼ cup batter). Place 1 tablespoon cream cheese mixture in center of each cup. Top evenly with remaining batter.

4. Bake 25 to 28 minutes or until toothpick inserted into centers comes out clean. Cool in pans 10 minutes. Remove to wire racks; cool completely.

5. Combine frosting and maple syrup in medium bowl until well blended. Frost cupcakes; garnish with orange peel.

Makes 14 jumbo cupcakes

DOUBLE PUMPKIN MUFFINS

2½ cups all-purpose flour	1 cup canned pumpkin
1 cup packed brown sugar	¾ cup milk
1 tablespoon baking powder	2 eggs
1 teaspoon ground cinnamon	6 tablespoons (¾ stick) butter, melted
½ teaspoon ground nutmeg	½ cup golden raisins
½ teaspoon ground ginger	⅔ cup roasted salted pumpkin seeds, divided
¼ teaspoon salt	

1. Preheat oven to 400°F. Line 16 standard (2½-inch) muffin cups with paper baking cups or spray with nonstick cooking spray.

2. Combine flour, brown sugar, baking powder, cinnamon, nutmeg, ginger and salt in large bowl; mix well. Combine pumpkin, milk, eggs and butter in medium bowl; beat until well blended. Add to flour mixture; stir just until dry ingredients are moistened. Stir in raisins and ⅓ cup pumpkin seeds. Spoon batter evenly into prepared muffin cups; sprinkle with remaining ⅓ cup pumpkin seeds.

3. Bake 15 to 18 minutes or until toothpick inserted into centers comes out clean. Cool in pans 10 minutes. Remove to wire racks; cool completely.

Makes 16 muffins

CARROT AND OAT MUFFINS

½ cup milk

½ cup unsweetened
  applesauce

2 eggs, beaten

1 tablespoon canola or
  vegetable oil

½ cup shredded carrot
  (1 medium to large carrot)

¾ cup plus 2 tablespoons
  old-fashioned oats

¾ cup all-purpose flour

¾ cup whole wheat flour

⅓ cup sugar

1½ teaspoons baking powder

1 teaspoon ground cinnamon

½ teaspoon baking soda

¼ teaspoon salt

¼ cup finely chopped walnuts
  (optional)

1. Preheat oven to 350°F. Spray 12 standard (2½-inch) muffin cups with nonstick cooking spray or line with paper baking cups.

2. Whisk milk, applesauce, eggs and oil in large bowl until blended. Stir in carrot. Combine oats, all-purpose flour, whole wheat flour, sugar, baking powder, cinnamon, baking soda and salt in medium bowl; mix well. Add flour mixture to applesauce mixture; stir just until batter is moistened. *(Do not overmix.)*

3. Spoon batter evenly into prepared muffin cups. Sprinkle 1 teaspoon walnuts over each muffin, if desired.

4. Bake 20 to 22 minutes or until golden brown. Cool in pan 5 minutes. Remove to wire rack; cool completely.

Makes 12 muffins

NOTE: These muffins are best eaten the day they're made.

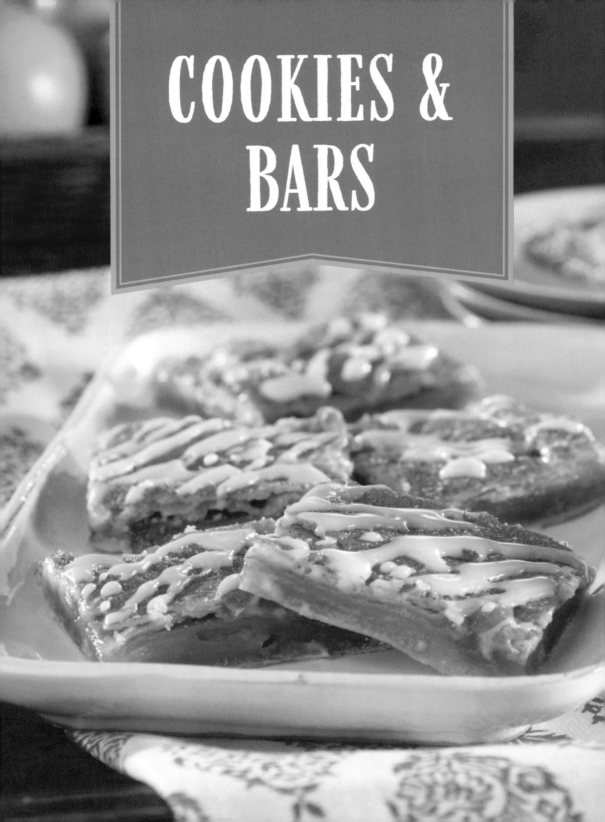

COOKIES & BARS

AUTUMN APPLE BARS

1 package (15 ounces) refrigerated pie crusts (2 crusts)

1 cup graham cracker crumbs

8 tart apples, peeled and sliced ¼ inch thick (8 cups)

1 cup plus 2 tablespoons granulated sugar, divided

2½ teaspoons ground cinnamon, divided

¼ teaspoon ground nutmeg

1 egg white

1 cup powdered sugar

1 to 2 tablespoons milk

½ teaspoon vanilla

1. Preheat oven to 350°F. Roll out one pie crust to 15×10-inch rectangle on lightly floured surface. Place in ungreased 15×10-inch baking pan.

2. Sprinkle graham cracker crumbs over dough; layer apple slices over crumbs. Combine 1 cup granulated sugar, 1½ teaspoons cinnamon and nutmeg in small bowl; sprinkle over apples.

3. Roll out remaining pie crust to 15×10-inch rectangle; place over apple layer. Beat egg white in small bowl until foamy; brush over top crust. Combine remaining 2 tablespoons granulated sugar and remaining 1 teaspoon cinnamon in separate small bowl; sprinkle over crust.

4. Bake 45 minutes or until lightly browned. Cool completely in pan on wire rack.

5. Combine powdered sugar, 1 tablespoon milk and vanilla in small bowl; stir until smooth. Add additional milk, if necessary, to reach desired consistency. Drizzle over bars.

Makes about 3 dozen bars

HARVEST PUMPKIN COOKIES

2 cups all-purpose flour	1 cup sugar
1 teaspoon baking powder	1 cup canned pumpkin
1 teaspoon ground cinnamon	1 egg
½ teaspoon baking soda	1 teaspoon vanilla
½ teaspoon salt	1 cup chopped pecans
½ teaspoon ground allspice	1 cup dried cranberries or raisins
1 cup (2 sticks) butter, softened	Pecan halves (about 36)

1. Preheat oven to 375°F. Combine flour, baking powder, cinnamon, baking soda, salt and allspice in medium bowl.

2. Beat butter and sugar in large bowl with electric mixer at medium speed until light and fluffy. Beat in pumpkin, egg and vanilla. Gradually add flour mixture, beating at low speed just until blended. Stir in chopped pecans and cranberries.

3. Drop heaping tablespoonfuls of dough 2 inches apart onto ungreased cookie sheets. Flatten slightly with back of spoon. Press one pecan half into center of each cookie.

4. Bake 10 to 12 minutes or until golden brown. Cool on cookie sheets 1 minute. Remove to wire racks; cool completely. Store tightly covered at room temperature or freeze up to 3 months.

Makes about 3 dozen cookies

CRANBERRY WALNUT GRANOLA BARS

2 packages (3 ounces each) ramen noodles, any flavor, broken into small pieces*

¾ cup all-purpose flour

1 teaspoon pumpkin pie spice

½ teaspoon baking soda

½ teaspoon salt

1 cup packed brown sugar

¼ cup (½ stick) butter, softened

2 eggs

¼ cup orange juice

1 cup chopped walnuts

½ cup dried cranberries

*Discard seasoning packets.

1. Preheat oven to 350°F. Spray 9-inch square baking pan with nonstick cooking spray.

2. Combine noodles, flour, pumpkin pie spice, baking soda and salt in medium bowl.

3. Beat brown sugar and butter in large bowl with electric mixer at medium speed 3 minutes or until light and fluffy. Add eggs and orange juice; beat until blended. Gradually add flour mixture, beating at low speed just until blended. Stir in walnuts and cranberries. Spread batter in prepared pan.

4. Bake 20 to 25 minutes or until toothpick inserted into center comes out clean. Cool completely before cutting into bars.

Makes 12 bars

CARAMEL APPLE BARS

2 cups all-purpose flour

1 teaspoon salt

½ teaspoon baking powder

½ teaspoon baking soda

⅔ cup (11 tablespoons) butter

¾ cup packed brown sugar

½ cup granulated sugar

1 egg

1 teaspoon vanilla

4 Granny Smith apples, peeled and coarsely chopped

½ cup pecans, chopped

24 caramel candies, unwrapped

2 tablespoons milk

1. Preheat oven to 350°F. Spray 13×9-inch baking pan with nonstick cooking spray.

2. Combine flour, salt, baking powder and baking soda in medium bowl. Melt butter in medium saucepan over medium heat. Remove from heat; stir in brown sugar and granulated sugar. Add egg and vanilla; stir until well blended. Add flour mixture; mix well. Press into bottom of prepared baking pan; top with apples.

3. Bake 40 to 45 minutes or until edges are browned and pulling away from sides of pan. Cool completely in pan on wire rack.

4. Toast pecans in medium nonstick skillet over medium-high heat 2 minutes or until fragrant, stirring frequently. Remove from skillet; set aside. Wipe out skillet with paper towel. Heat caramels and milk in same skillet over medium-low heat until melted and smooth, stirring constantly.

5. Drizzle caramel sauce over cooled apple bars; sprinkle with pecans. Let stand 30 minutes before cutting.

Makes 2 to 3 dozen bars

PUMPKIN SWIRL BROWNIES

Pumpkin Swirl

- **4 ounces cream cheese, softened**
- **½ cup canned pumpkin**
- **1 egg**
- **3 tablespoons sugar**
- **¾ teaspoon pumpkin pie spice**
- **Pinch salt**

Brownies

- **½ cup (1 stick) butter**
- **6 ounces semisweet chocolate, chopped**
- **1 cup sugar**
- **3 eggs**
- **1 teaspoon vanilla**
- **¾ cup all-purpose flour**
- **2 tablespoons unsweetened cocoa powder**
- **½ teaspoon salt**

1. Preheat oven to 350°F. Spray 8-inch square baking pan with nonstick cooking spray or line with parchment paper.

2. For pumpkin swirl, combine cream cheese, pumpkin, 1 egg, 3 tablespoons sugar, pumpkin pie spice and pinch of salt in medium bowl; beat until smooth.

3. For brownies, melt butter and chocolate in medium saucepan over low heat, stirring frequently. Remove from heat; stir in 1 cup sugar until blended. Beat in 3 eggs, one at a time, until well blended. Stir in vanilla. Add flour, cocoa and ½ teaspoon salt; stir until blended. Reserve ⅓ cup brownie batter in small bowl; spread remaining batter in prepared pan.

4. Spread pumpkin mixture evenly over brownie batter. Drop reserved brownie batter by teaspoonfuls over pumpkin layer; draw tip of knife through top of both batters to marbleize. (If reserved brownie batter has become very thick upon standing, microwave on LOW (30%) 20 to 30 seconds or until loosened, stirring at 10-second intervals.)

5. Bake 28 to 30 minutes or just until center is set and edges begin to pull away from sides of pan. (Toothpick will come out with fudgy crumbs.) Cool in pan on wire rack.

Makes about 16 brownies

SWEET POTATO COCONUT BARS

30 shortbread cookies, crushed

1¼ cups finely chopped walnuts, toasted,* divided

¾ cup sweetened flaked coconut, divided

¼ cup (½ stick) butter, softened

2 cans (16 ounces each) sweet potatoes, well drained and mashed (2 cups)

2 eggs

1 teaspoon ground cinnamon

½ teaspoon ground ginger

¼ teaspoon ground cloves

¼ teaspoon salt

1 can (14 ounces) sweetened condensed milk

¾ cup butterscotch chips

*To toast walnuts, spread in single layer on baking sheet. Bake in preheated 350°F oven 8 to 10 minutes or until golden brown, stirring frequently.

1. Preheat oven to 350°F.

2. Combine cookie crumbs, 1 cup walnuts, ½ cup coconut and butter in food processor; process using on/off pulses until well combined. Press two thirds of mixture onto bottom of 8-inch square baking pan.

3. Beat sweet potatoes, eggs, cinnamon, ginger, cloves and salt in large bowl with electric mixer at medium-low speed until well blended. Gradually add sweetened condensed milk, beating at low speed until well blended. Spoon filling evenly over prepared crust. Sprinkle with remaining crumb mixture.

4. Bake 45 to 50 minutes or until knife inserted into center comes out clean. Sprinkle evenly with butterscotch chips, remaining ¼ cup walnuts and ¼ cup coconut. Bake 5 minutes. Cool completely in pan on wire rack. Cover and refrigerate 2 hours before serving.

Makes 16 bars

PEAR HAZELNUT BARS

¾ cup (1½ sticks) butter, softened

¾ cup plus 2 tablespoons granulated sugar, divided

1 tablespoon plus 1 teaspoon grated lemon peel, divided

3 egg yolks

1 teaspoon vanilla

2 cups plus 2 tablespoons all-purpose flour, divided

¼ teaspoon salt

4 cups chopped peeled pears

½ cup raisins

2 tablespoons fresh lemon juice

½ teaspoon ground cinnamon

Crumb Topping

½ cup all-purpose flour

½ cup packed brown sugar

½ teaspoon ground cinnamon

½ cup (1 stick) cold butter, cut into small pieces

½ cup old-fashioned oats

½ cup chopped hazelnuts

1. Preheat oven to 350°F. Line 13×9-inch baking pan with foil, leaving 1-inch overhang. Spray foil with nonstick cooking spray.

2. Beat ¾ cup butter, ¾ cup granulated sugar and 1 tablespoon lemon peel in large bowl with electric mixer at medium speed 1 minute. Beat in egg yolks and vanilla until well blended. Add 2 cups flour and ¼ teaspoon salt; beat just until combined. Press dough evenly into prepared pan. Bake 25 minutes or until lightly browned. Set pan aside on wire rack.

3. Meanwhile, mix pears, raisins, lemon juice, ½ teaspoon cinnamon, remaining 2 tablespoons flour, 2 tablespoons granulated sugar and 1 teaspoon lemon peel in large bowl. Arrange over warm crust.

4. For topping, combine ½ cup flour, brown sugar and ½ teaspoon cinnamon in medium bowl. Cut in ½ cup butter with pastry blender or electric mixer at low speed until mixture resembles coarse crumbs. Stir in oats and hazelnuts. Sprinkle topping evenly over filling, pressing lightly.

5. Bake 30 to 32 minutes or until topping is bubbly and golden brown. Cool completely on wire rack. Refrigerate bars at least 2 hours before serving. Remove foil from bars; cut into squares. Cut each square diagonally into triangles. Store covered in refrigerator.

Makes 3 dozen bars

WHOLE WHEAT PUMPKIN BARS

- 1 cup all-purpose flour
- 1 cup whole wheat flour
- ¾ cup sugar
- 1½ teaspoons baking powder
- 1½ teaspoons ground cinnamon
- 1 teaspoon baking soda
- ¾ teaspoon salt
- ½ teaspoon ground ginger
- ½ teaspoon ground nutmeg
- 1 can (15 ounces) pumpkin
- ¾ cup canola or vegetable oil
- 2 eggs
- 2 tablespoons molasses
- Cream Cheese Frosting (recipe follows)
- ½ cup mini semisweet chocolate chips

1. Preheat oven to 350°F. Spray 13×9-inch baking pan with nonstick cooking spray.

2. Combine all-purpose flour, whole wheat flour, sugar, baking powder, cinnamon, baking soda, salt, ginger and nutmeg in medium bowl; mix well. Whisk pumpkin, oil, eggs and molasses in large bowl until well blended. Add flour mixture; stir until blended. Spread batter in prepared pan. (Batter will be very thick.)

3. Bake 20 to 25 minutes or until toothpick inserted into center comes out clean. Cool completely in pan on wire rack.

4. Prepare Cream Cheese Frosting. Spread frosting over bars; sprinkle with chocolate chips.

Makes 2 to 3 dozen bars

CREAM CHEESE FROSTING: Beat 4 ounces softened cream cheese and ½ cup (1 stick) softened butter in medium bowl with electric mixer at medium-high speed until creamy. Add 2 cups powdered sugar; beat at low speed until blended. Add 1 tablespoon milk; beat at medium-high speed 2 to 3 minutes or until frosting is light and fluffy.

Index